STIMULATING AWARENESS

ABOUT LIFE

Cecelia Frances Page

iUniverse, Inc.
New York   Bloomington

STIMULATING AWARENESS ABOUT LIFE

iUniverse books may be ordered through booksellers or by contacting:

iUniverse
1663 Liberty Drive
Bloomington, IN 47403
www.iuniverse.com
1-800-Authors (1-800-288-4677)

ISBN: 978-1-4502-1928-0 (sc)
ISBN: 978-1-4502-1929-7 (e-book)

Printed in the United States of America

iUniverse rev. date:. 4/8/2010

Contents

Cecelia Frances Page

Preface

STIMULATING AWARENESS ABOUT LIFE is an invigorating book with 65 worthwhile topics. HUMAN INTEREST topics are Sunny Acres For Homeless People, Unhappy and Happy Feelings, The Christmas Gift, Living In A Mountain Cabin, The Unfaithful Partner, How Modern Conveniences Affect Us, Why People Gossip and Picnic At The Lake. SOCIAL AND POLITICAL topics are Aztecs From Mexico, World Government, The Causes Of War, Aggression Of The Taliban, Political Propaganda, Conspiracies In The World, Old Fashion Customs, Making Enemies Our Friends and Fragile Relationships.

RELIGIOUS AND PHILOSOPHICAL topics are Important Spiritual Leaders, The Fourth Dimension, Daily Meditation, The Cosmic Christ, The Theosophical Society, Wisdom Within, The True Mission Of Jesus Christ, The Star Of Bethlehem, Chohans Of The Seven Rays, The Knights Templar, The Philosophy Of Dolores Cannon, The Golden City, The Sacred Chalice, Significant Visions, Morality Versus Immortality, The Special Message, Awaken To Spiritual Consciousness and Twin Flames.

UFO, SCIENCE AND HEALTH topics are The Magic Of Spring, Better Ways To Control Diabetes, Exercise Your Body, UFO Sightings Described In The Bible, UFO Underground Bases, Jupiter, Our Second Sun, Intelligent Beings From The Pleiades, What Is Happening To Coral Sea Beds?, Causes Of Global Warming, The Need For Clean Water, The Enormous Sea Turtle, The Need For Electric Cars, Other Planets In Outer Space, Life At A Lagoon, Keep Care Of Your Teeth, How To Live In Harmony With Nature and Life As A Vegan. OTHER TOPICS are Steve Omar's Experiences As A Surfer, Actions And Reactions,

Florida's Stonehenge, Our Ancient Ancestors, Flamenco Dancers, Life On A Submarine, Progressive Methods Of Education, Cable Television, Underground Shelters, Seafood Dishes, How Scammers Fool People and Chinese New Year.

About The Author

Cecelia Frances Page is an author who has written 50 books. Eight books are self published. 42 books are published by iUniverse Incorporated. Cecelia Frances Page has been writing poetry, short stories, articles and research papers since the age of 19. Cecelia has a B.A. and M.A. in Education. She has focused in English, Speech, Drama and Psychology. Cecelia has published five screenplays and three original, poetry books. Cecelia is an educator, writer, pianist, vocal soloist, piano and vocal teacher, philosopher, stage play director, photographer and artist.

The names of Cecelia Frances Page's books are *Westward Pursuits, Opportune Times, Imagine If…, Power Of Creative And Worthwhile Living, Fortunately, Certain People Make A Difference, New Perspectives, Celestial Connections, Celestial Beings From Outer Space, Awesome Episodes, Vivid Memories of Halcyon, Phenomenal Experiences, Expand Your Awareness, Adventures On Ancient Continents, Awaken To Spiritual Illumination, Seek Enlightenment Within, Brilliant Candor, Fascinating Topics, Very Worthwhile Endeavors And Circumstances, Horizons Beyond, Pathways to Spiritual Realization, Mystical Realities, Magnificent Celestial Journeys, Extraordinary Encounters, Incredible Times, Tremendous Moments, Amazing Stories and Articles, Adventurous Experiences, Extraterrestrial Civilizations On Earth, Relevant Interests, Impressionable Occurrences, Interpretations Of Life, Tangible Realities, Remarkable World Travels, The Future Age Beyond The New Age Movement, Infinite Opportunities, Immense Possibilities, Significant Moments, Random Selections, Marvelous Reflections, Stimulating Awareness About Life* and more.

Cecelia Frances Page continues to write books to inspire others and to encourage her readers to be creative, productive human beings. You can order any of her books at iUniverse Incorporated at 1-800-288-4677, Extension 5025.

Nonfiction

ONE

Important Spiritual Leaders

Gautama Buddha lived approximately five hundred years before Jesus Christ. He became the desireless Buddha. Gautama Buddha sat under a Bo tree in India to become awakened to spiritual truths and enlightenment. He found bliss and peace as he awakened to eternal truths and universal love. He detached himself from worldly ways in order to seek wisdom and purification.

Gautama Buddha developed an eight fold path. He focused on right action, right concentration, right association, right occupation, right meditation, right morality, right thinking and right health. Buddha's spiritual leadership has changed many Asians into responsible followers of Buddha and his eight fold path. Buddhism has spread around the world. As a result, more people are enlightened and are living better lives.

St. Germaine has influenced many followers to practice self transformation by applying alchemy. Followers learn to transmute wrong-doing and misqualified energies. St. Germaine became a spiritual leader because he focused on laws of transmutation to promote harmony, balance and equilibrium.

St. Germaine stated, "The now of the present hour must be utilized as a chalice of spiritual opportunity. The power to change is within every man. Each man must become aware of his choices and select either freedom or fetters as he explores the chemistry of his present state, brings it into focus upon the mirror of truth, and then determines to alter each base condition, constructing within the crucible of the hour that hollowed progress which is born of the eternal perception." St. Germaine said, "Only God can bring eternal satisfaction to the whole Earth."

St. Germaine has helped to change the world with his spiritual leadership. He has influenced early American leaders when America was being formed. He protected George Washington, America's first president.

Paramahamsa Sri Nithyanda (Swamiji) is a truly revolutionary, spiritual master and leader of our century. Swami embarked upon his spiritual journey at a very young age. He traveled the length and breadth of India on foot studying with great masters in India and Nepal and practicing intense meditation with extraordinary vigor. He experienced the final flowering of consciousness on January 1, 2000 when he entered into a state of ultimate bliss.

With a pragmatic yet compassionate approach to life and spirituality and an enlightened insight into the care of human nature, Swami has reached out to touch millions of hearts across the world. Swamiji's mission is simple—to awaken the divinity that lies latent in man.

Dhyanapeetam, the worldwide movement for meditation, was born of this vision on January 1, 2003. With its spiritual nerve centre in Bidadi (near Bangalore in India) has over 300 centers around the world. Dhyanapeetam works towards the transformation of humanity through the inner transformation of the individual. Swamiji's divine healing powers and simple, practical meditation techniques help you blossom in every sphere of life---be it physical, emotional, intellectual or spiritual. Breathing techniques and chanting are used. Silencing the mind is applied to calm the mind.

Swami Paramahamsa Sri Nithyanda has made a spiritual difference because of his spiritual leadership around the world. He awakens and enlightens many people while he travels from one place to another place.

The teachings of Maitreya are described in THE LAW OF LIFE, edited by Benjamin Crème. Lord Maitreya inspires everyone through mind, spiritual and body to generate self-respect, out of which the blessings of salvation will emerge, which will make life meaningful for one and all.

Benjamin Crème said, "The present political system is fast undergoing changes inspired by Maitreya. In short, each and every country will generate self respect and let each and every nation enjoy the fruits of life.

Whatever you see in the world of suffering, crime and violence will begin to disappear in a short space of time."

Ron Hubbard has developed Scientology, the Science of Dianetics which is the modern science of Mental Health. Ron Hubbard has changed the world because many followers of Scientology experience clearances. Individuals learn to evaluate and transmute traumatic experiences by being interviewed. Individuals are transformed by applying Scientology procedures to overcome negative, memory banks in their subconscious. We are freed from anger, hatred, prejudices, violent habits and negative memory banks. Ron Hubbard became a world, spiritual leader, who has changed the world because of his progressive methods of clearing people emotionally, mentally as well as physically.

One of the most important spiritual leaders in the world was Jesus Christ. Jesus was born near Bethlehem approximately two thousand years ago. Jesus taught his followers to live by the Golden Rule. The Golden Rule is to treat others as you would like to be treated. Jesus forgave humanity when he was on the cross of crucifixion. He set an example by living by brotherhood, service and good will to humanity. Jesus was kind, benevolent and caring about others. He was able to heal many people as long as they had faith in being healed of their afflictions and illnesses.

Jesus Christ has helped humanity to awaken to truth and wisdom. He sacrificed his life to serve others. He was the greatest teacher and Master because he lived the truth and taught others how to know God and to become aware of the Real Self known as the Christ Self. He said, "I Am One with the Father." Jesus focused on promoting peace and harmony in the world.

TWO

The Magic Of Spring

The magic of spring exists when new life is blossoming in the plant kingdom. When animals, birds and human beings are born new life brings joy and renewing of living things. Each seed that germinates in the ground grows into one of God's creations.

Observe a flower grow into a beautiful, colorful blossom with spreading pedals and green leaves. Each new flower adds to a garden. A variety of colors emanate in the flower beds. New flowers add to the beauty of each garden.

Many wild flowers blossom in meadows and fields such as lupines, poppies, sour grass, pink ladies and sunflowers. Wild flowers grow profusely in many fields and meadows across the countryside. The magic of a rose is magnificent to enjoy. Pedals spiral into a splendid design. Tulips unfold into colorful designs. Tulips grow close together and spread around a garden with many colors. Daisies radiate light from their centers. Pedals spread out from their golden centers. Pansies have a velvety texture. Their fragrance adds to nature's décor.

Evergreen trees sprout in many places. Their healing fragrance uplifts passer-bys. Their green needles last with a verdant green light. Evergreen trees produce cones. The cones contain seeds to produce new trees. There are pine, spruce, fir, silver pine and redwood trees. Evergreen trees add to the magic of spring.

Moss and lichen grow on trees in forests. Lichen hangs down on tree branches. Moss grows around the base of trees. Four-leaf clovers grow and spread in fields, gardens and meadows creating a green, magical appearance especially during springtime.

Springtime is a time for new baby birds to hatch. It is a time for fawns to be born. Baby squirrels, rabbits, opossums, foxes, bears, elk, moose and many more animals are born in the spring. These newborn creatures depend on their mothers to take care of them until they are able to become independent and able to care for themselves.

Baby mammals suckle milk from their mothers. They usually cling to their mothers to keep warm and safe while they are young. As they grow up they become less dependent on their parents. They learn to find food and water. They learn how to survive by observing their parents.

Whales, seals, otters, walruses, manatees and dolphins are mammals. Baby sea creatures also suckle milk from their mothers. Baby whales, seals, otters, walruses, manatees and dolphins follow their parents in the ocean. Seals, otters and walruses stay on icebergs to rest. They sun themselves during daytime.

Baby birds usually stay in bird nests until they can fly. Baby birds hatch out of shells. They depend on their parents to feed them while they are still in the nests. Without their parents to feed them, baby birds would not survive. In time, they learn to search for food after they learn to fly. There are many birds around the world.

Other mammals are lions, tigers, leopards, cheetahs, elephants, monkeys, apes, sloths, anteaters, hyenas, gazelles, rhinos and hippopotami. Their babies also suckle milk. They follow their parents. They need protection when they are growing up. As they observe their parents they learn how to survive.

New life forms continue to be born and to grow especially during springtime. Spring is a magical time to observe new life.

THREE

Better Ways To Control Diabetes

Diabetes can be controlled by taking oligomeric proanlhocyanadins twice a day in powder form with 5 ounces of water each time. The powder contains grape seed, green tea, pine bark and red wine extracts along with lemon bioflavonoids, resveratrol and 23 naturally occurring vitamins and enzymes.

Anyone who has kidney failure may not be able to take OPC Factor because their kidneys will not be able to process the vitamins and chemicals. They may have severe headaches.

Essentials OPC Factor is the first 100% organic formula fueled by a revolutionary high speed "liquid" delivery system that mimics the body's natural pH. This provides an amazing 97% absorption rate.

"Pills and tablets have absorption rates as low as 2 to 20 percent," said Dr. Charles Berg. "Actual blood scans taken twenty minutes apart show how OPC Factor virtually flushes away free radicals, excess cholesterol crystals and sugar molecules in the bloodstream."

Excess sugar in one's blood causes oxidation which leads to "slow sticky blood," a problem linked to neuropathy and edema in extremities as well as kidney damage and even blindness. OPC Factor greatly improves circulation promoting faster blood flow crucial for diabetics.

Charles Leavitt of Louisiana said, "OPC Factor has helped lower my glucose levels. I sleep better and have more energy and better circulation."

The NIH Study proves that the OPC Factor works. He said, "I can feel it when I drink it. It gives a lot of energy."

A National Institute of Health funded "Double Blind" clinical study published in July, 2008 supports customer claims about energy for diabetics. "Energy equals better sleep, moods and overall balance."

Dr. Charles Berg said, "Studies have found that free radicals produce oxidation that disrupts insulin. OPC Factor works 20-50 times better than traditional anti-oxidants against oxidation." OPC enhances insulin's ability to lower blood sugar.

Jacki Rolph, a diabetic from Idaho Falls said, "If you get this product, try it. I have been diabetic 48 years. OPC Factor helped decrease my insulin by a third. I have my life back!"

You can receive a free book entitled THE AGING ANTIDOTE which usually costs $20 if you purchase OFC Factor risk-free today and receive a free 30-Day Bonus supply. Call 1-800-845-2603. OFC Factor washes away blood sludge by eliminating toxins, free radicals and even parasites.

FOUR

Sunny Acres For Homeless People

Sunny Acres has been in operation for nine years. It is owned by Dan De Vaul in San Luis Obispo County in California. It is the only place in San Luis Obispo County that provides a "long-term" living situation for people who were formerly homeless.

In addition, people who come to Sunny Acres to live are provided with three hot meals a day. 12-step recovery meetings held twice weekly, and a unique opportunity to rehabilitate at a pace that works for each on an individual basis. This is accomplished in large part by working on these 72 acres and on 10 acres of it specifically. Homeless people work on the ranch and perform such jobs as growing crops, dealing with the 40 head of cattle, repairing and maintaining farm equipment, automobile mechanics, and restoration, welding, converting wine barrels into water barrels and more. Training is provided as needed to those who show interest in a particular area.

All of these jobs provide hands on rehabilitation that helps those who are getting sober to stay sober as well as building their self esteem. Each resident is treated as an individual with their own strengths and weaknesses taken into consideration when they are admitted to Sunny Acres.

Sunny Acres operates like a big family. A balance of time, talents and personalities has created an environment that works. Residents find their dignity has been restored and they respect one another.

$300 is asked by those who can afford it. Those who can't afford to pay compensate by working enough hours to make up for their expenses at Sunny Acres. Five volunteer hours a week are required by residents.

After Sunny Acres organization was established as a nonprofit organization it was decided that Sunny Acres would pay a rental fee of $4,000 per month to Dan De Vaul. To this day that fee has never been collected. In fact, during the first seven years of Sunny Acres operation, Dan De Vaul supplemented the nonprofit program with his own funds to keep it going. It is only during the past two years that the program has become fully, financially self sustaining.

Sunny Acres has never requested or received any government subsidies or tax dollars. The Food Bank Coalition of San Luis Obispo generously supplies residents some of their food. The rest of the food is grown on the farm. Monetary donations as well as clothing and other needed items have been received from many community members and businesses.

County-run agencies have often referred many of the men and women who have come to stay at Sunny Acres. People working in these agencies have seen first hand this good work. Dan De Vaul envisioned 10 of his 72 acres devoted to the homeless with the rest being developed in three tires, beginning with some affordable housing.

San Luis Obispo County has adopted a ten year plan to end homelessness. Sunny Acres is uniquely positioned to help achieve this goal.

In November, 2009 Dan De Vaul was arrested because of the County's Land Department accusing him of electrical wiring and building code violations in trailer homes. He was sent to jail. Someone paid bail to get him out of jail. He has to pay expensive fines. The County of San Luis Obispo agencies should help to pay for electrical wiring required to use electricity at Sunny Acres. Sunny Acres should be kept open to help provide a place for homeless individuals to live.

If all the taxpayers funds in the County government used to pay inspectors, police, a judge, jury, court officials, clerks, secretaries and others included in this case had been used to make the facility legal---it would not have been necessary to arrest and prosecute Dan De Vaul. This case dragged on for a few years at substantial expense. Why not use these funds to help the homeless and hungry? The inspectors charged the facilities were dangerous. However, a reporter who investigated this case stated that there was no evidence of any injuries or harm on this land all those years.

Nonfiction

FIVE

The Fourth Dimension

The Fourth Dimension is invisible to the physical eyes. This invisible dimension is on a much higher vibration and frequency. Life in the Fourth Dimension is magnificent. This dimension can be seen with the astral eyes.

Life in the Fourth Dimension is harmonious and blissful. Spirit beings move about freely in flowing light. The Fourth Dimension is parallel to the physical plane. Spirit beings serve and continue to learn about spiritual laws and Cosmic principles.

Ascended Masters work with souls in the Fourth Dimension to help them evolve spiritually. Pastel colors of pink, violet, gold, green, blue and white are blazing and swirling in this Fourth Dimension. Spirit beings exist in harmony and peace. They communicate in their astral forms.

Celestial melodies can be heard in the Fourth Dimension. These cosmic melodies cause life to maintain harmony. Flowers communicate with passer-bys. They have consciousness and flowers respond with one another.

Celestial spirits communicate with mental telepathy. They think faster and respond swifter with others. Celestial spirits can travel around quickly in the Fourth Dimension.

In the Fourth Dimension time has become timeless. A soul may be in the Fourth Dimension for a long time. Yet, the soul doesn't experience a feeling of time and doesn't experience human suffering. A soul can experience a blissful state of awareness.

SIX

Steve Omar's Experiences As A Surfer

Steve Omar has been surfing since he was thirteen in San Clemente, California. Steve's neighbor and friend, Nancy Nelson, was a three time World Contest winner who influenced him to begin surfing. Steve was impressed because Nancy surfed in big waves in Hawaii at age 13 and won the World Contest at a young age.

Steve taught himself to surf, including the 40 different tricks and maneuvers done by the best surfers in the world then. Omar invented six new surfing maneuvers which were unknown in contests. Steve never took surf lessons and learned by trial and error. Eventually, his room mates were World Champion and National Champion surfers with influence.

At 15, Steve successfully rode the biggest waves of anyone in his high school. This school was known for surfing champions. Learning to surf was very dangerous and challenging. Steve learned to surf through a pier with dangerous pilings and barnacles that destroyed surfboards.

The biggest surf Steve ever saw in California arrived when he was 15. The storm waves were breaking to the top of a pier that was estimated to be 40 feet high, washed over the Pacific Coast Highway and flooded numerous beach homes. Omar surfed a few days on this kind of surf and rode some waves to shore without falling. The faces of a few of those waves were estimated 25 to 30 feet high.

During the winter the fog became very thick. Surfers couldn't see waves moving toward them or the beach. Big waves came out of the fog to crash on the surfers paddling out. Sometimes the fog was so thick that the surfers wiped out on waves, lost their surfboards in the currents and could not locate them on the beach. They hiked the beach to find their surfboards. Sometimes the surfers drifted for hours in the fog and arrived on shore at a different beach. Another wipeout was crashing into rocks and boulders in the fog. Surfers also crashed into piers and other surfers.

Steve Omar surfed without a wetsuit. Sometimes it was so cold that hail was dropping down on surfers. The morning air dropped down in the 40s and the ocean was in the 50s. Cold, strong winds blew on the surfers. Surfers did not have safety leashes in those days and had to swim all the way to shore in cold water after wipeouts. They would get lost in the fog and get sucked into rocky cliffs and boulders by rip tides. Many surfboards were destroyed in these conditions. Most surfers didn't have wetsuits in those days. When wetsuits were invented for surfers they leaked in cold water, were poorly insulated and left the wearer shivering.

Surfing music became the most popular, rock music in California in the early 1960s. Surfing fashions and culture was a huge fad in Steve's high school. In his senior year, Steve led his baseball team in home runs and hit in the winning run in the All Star Game. Yet, Steve gave up baseball for surfing and never played it again. Riding big waves was more exciting.

Steve bought his first surfboard after mowing lawns for 25 cents for months. The used board was damaged. Unable to afford new surfboards and repairs, Steve began a small surfboard making and patching business at age 15. School friends saw these hand-made surfboards and wanted to purchase. Omar Surfboards began and provided money for a 1,400 mile surf trip into Mexico and to Hawaii to ride the big surf. The surfboard business began in a garage and eventually a surf shop was built in Puerto Rico. Omar Surfboards were also expanded to Oahu and a few surfboards were made on Maui. The emphasis was on quality and innovation rather than quantity. Trained co-workers eventually made most Omar Surfboards. One winter the man who won the International Surfing Championships surfed on an Omar Surfboard.

At the age of 16 Steve Omar traveled alone to Hawaii to ride big waves. He didn't have a place to stay when he got to Hawaii and did not know anyone to meet at the airport. He was lucky to get a seat on the flight right next to 12 year old Peter Johnson who was also alone. This little kid said he was going to right the big surf on the North Shore of Oahu. Peter also said he would be picked up at the airport by the Number One rated surfer in the world, Phil Edwards. Omar was skeptical of those claims.

When Steve Omar and Peter Johnson got off the plane at the airport, Peter introduced him to his friend, Phil Edwards. Phil was a big hero to Omar so this was a great surprise. Phil was very friendly. He gave Steve instructions about how to get into Waikiki and get a room and gave valuable directions.

The following year Steve saw a surfing movie in a movie theater entitled THE ENDLESS SUMMER. The movie showed 12 year old Peter Johnson successfully surfing the beach with the biggest surfing waves in the whole world! The action took place at dangerous Waimea Bay where the best surfers took terrible wipeouts. Peter went on to become a big surf star.

Many years later Phil Edwards showed up on Maui and requested a sailboard lesson from Steve Omar. Many of the best surfers wanted to learn to windsurf in those days and Omar had become an expert sailboarder. Steve gave him a free lesson on his simulator and they had lunch in a restaurant and discussed old times.

Steve got tired of the small waves in Waikiki and hitch-hiked to the North Shore where the biggest surfing waves in the world were located. He went to Sunset Beach where the big wave contests were held. He slept on the beach on top of his surfboard the first night. Steve surfed there for five days and performed well.

Three famous surf stars were impressed with Steve's hand-made surfboard. They were on the covers of surf magazines and starred in movies. These guys gave Omar a free room in their beach home at Sunset Beach, all free meals and rides to surf spots. Pipeline was then considered the best shaped surfing wave in the world. One of these room mates was known as Mr. Pipeline from that winter. Another was the United States Surfing Champion. Another room mate became known as Mr. Sunset, the legendary star at Sunset Beach. For a 16 year old kid these surfers were really exciting.

Pipeline was also known as "the most dangerous surf in the world!" Several surfers were killed at Pipeline. It took great courage just to paddle out. The waves were so powerful they broke surfboards in half. Imagine what this surf could do to your bones and back! It was common to see bloody surfers emerging from the water. One friend broke his arm. The fronts of these waves got 30 to 40 feet high. The problem was that the big waves crashed on coral as sharp as razor blades in water that was only waist deep at low tide! Imagine getting thrown off the top of a wave and landing head first! An underwater cave was made out of sharp coral. One surfer got trapped in this cave and his skeleton was found in it years afterwards.

One surf movie maker was quoted saying, "The waves at Pipeline do not break. They explode."

Omar had never seen such powerful and dangerous waves. Surf stars were wiping out all day and broken surfboards were lying on the beach. A surfer named Peter Troy was covered with bandages from the top of his head to his toes over his entire body. He was called "The Living Mummy." This guy had been washed across a reef. For the first time Steve was too scared to paddle out.

However, a famous surf movie maker said he had some film left he wanted to use up and talked Omar into paddling out. After some wipeouts just trying to paddle out Steve found himself surrounded by surf stars getting pounded. Only rarely did anyone complete a ride. Surfers only had longboards in those days and it was easy to wipeout at Pipeline. Most wipeouts were going down the wave. Yet, Steve made it all the way to the bottom of a wave, turned and got a nice tube ride. However, after the tube ride the end of the wave caved in on Omar. This wipeout was enough to end the day of surfing.

Pipeline had the most dangerous surf but Waimea had the biggest surf in the world. The biggest days were reported over 50 feet in 1969 when surf destroyed many houses and part of the coast highway. Steve did not surf Waimea on his first trip but decided to try in 1969. That day dozens of surfers were watching from the beach but wouldn't paddle out. So Steve paddled out alone through a big, dangerous, crashing shore break right on the beach. He struggled to get past these dangerous waves. He saw the biggest surfing waves he had ever seen. When he caught a wave he had to make a quick, right turn. Directly in front of where surfers caught the waves was a point covered with big, dangerous boulders. The whitewater was big and crashing into those rocks. If a surfer failed to make the right turn or fell off the waves would try to push the victim into the boulders.

At the end of the ride was the most powerful riptide Steve had ever seen. It was like a river sucking surfers and surfboards a mile out into the ocean. A magazine told of sharks out there waiting for the many surfers who got dragged out. Usually a rescue boat or helicopter was out there to rescue surfers on big days. However, Steve got there early and there was nobody to rescue anybody.

Surfers also told of hitting the bottom of the ocean in water over 30 feet deep and being spun around like a giant washing machine. After too many spins a surfer could not tell which way was up or down. One surfer thought he was swimming up toward the surface and hit his head on the rocky bottom! It was very dark at that depth. Surfers told of being held underwater while five or ten waves rolled over before surfacing!

Steve had trained by swimming the entire length of a big, municipal swimming pool underwater, roundtrip and without surfacing. Yet, the biggest wave he had ever seen broke on him while paddling out. It seemed like an estimated half mile from shore. This experience was the closest to drowning of this career. After a long swim and recovering the surfboard it was time to catch a wave. Steve turned right, made it past the boulders, and angle across the wave toward the riptide. Then the big wave caved in and caused a bad wipeout. The swim in is the scariest part of Waimea Bay. A surfer must aim for a very narrow patch of sandy beach located between the boulders and the riptide. While struggling through big, crashing waves rolling in judgment and skill must be precise. A slight error to the left and a surfer gets pounded on the boulders where people have been killed. A slight error to the right and a surfer gets sucked a mile out to sea in the riptide. Steve struggled and barely made it to shore. He felt lucky to be alive. In spite of these wipeouts at Pipeline and Waimea Bay, Omar was determined to practice and progress at big wave surfing in the years to come.

The famous surf movie THE ENDLESS SUMMER inspired surfers to travel the world having adventures, excitement, romance, fun, paradises and good times. Steve traveled to Europe, North Africa, Australia, New Zealand, Fiji, Tahiti, Moorea, The Bahamas, Florida, Kauai, Lanai, Bali, Mexico, Peru and other places experiencing this lifestyle and searching for perfect waves. He even saw surf in Egypt. One trip was from California overland to Panama and included Costa Rica. Most of these travels were good times that were so much fun it is hard to put it in words. Steve calls it "living the dream."

Steve moved to Maui in 1967. In 1982 Hurricane Iwa smashed into the Hawaiian Islands and pounded Maui with monster surf. The big waves sank boats, wiped out highways and smashed into homes and parks. Omar and a couple of friends surfed the waves off the Lahaina Breakwater. Some of this surf was so big it went over the top of the breakwater and crashed into boats inside the harbor. Boats that had been offshore were smashed into the coastline. This surfing day was successful and Steve got many great rides.

Another day the Lahaina surf was so huge that it broke all the way across the harbor entrance so the boats could not sail in or out. More waves broke over the breakwater and sprayed boats. Only one surfer had even managed to get out to the surf. Steve made it out too and got a big wave and got a long ride. A wipeout would have resulted in being smashed into the harbor boulders.

Steve Omar received the lead star part in three surfing movies. He directed, cast and wrote the screenplays for some other surfing movies. Some of these surf movies were on television on Maui and all of them had some screen showing for audiences. Steve also got a couple of good waves on national television.

Omar was the founder and president of the Maui Surfing Association, produced and directed surf contests, was a pro contest judge and created the first all women and all kids contests on Maui.

Steve owned two surf schools and managed several others. One was his Maui Surfing Safaris which took tourists on adventure, surfing, hiking, scenic and sightseeing trips on Maui. He authored a surfing instruction manual and taught levels from beginner to pro. Steve coached some surfers who won contests.

In 1989 to 1999, Steve was the editor, publisher and chief writer for MAUI SURFING Magazine. He also covered Maui surfing contests for SURFER Magazine for awhile and had surfing columns in several Maui newspapers. Omar wrote some stories for some of the world's major surfing magazines. One of these magazines published a slick, full color special issue called OMAR'S STORY, which detailed his surfing experiences and histories in the 1960s to 1970s. This magazine was sold in international airports, super markets, pharmacies, surf shops and other magazines racks across the United States and Hawaii. This magazine reportedly "sold out."

Many surfers concluded that the shorter a surfboard is the more difficult to ride. Steve was photographed surfing his 3 feet, 11inch surfboard. As far as he could discover this was the shortest surfboard in the world.

Eventually Steve gave up big wave riding after being severely injured three times and rushed to the emergency rooms, and a few near drownings. He concluded that doing tricks while enjoying small waves was far more fun! Steve surfed small waves for many years with no injuries and all fun.

From 1977 to 2006, Steve was a Hawaii "beach boy" who was paid to go to the beach and surf. There were countless hours on tropical beaches playing guitar while making money renting out surfboards and selling surf lessons. While teaching surf lessons the instructors earned money giving surfing demonstrations to tourists. It was often fun to go in the warm ocean and surf with the students. It was even more fun to be paid to take tourists in a van on a surfing adventure safari on Maui to waterfalls, jungles, deserted tropical beaches and paradises.

Due to all the appearances in newspapers, magazines, surf movies and other media Steve never had to enter a contest to get sponsors. He got free surfboards, sportswear and accessories from sponsors. Steve preferred to produce contests rather than enter. By then Steve excelled on short boards.

In the 1990s a newly discovered surf break called Jaws was surfed on Maui. Jaws is an even bigger surf than Waimea Bay. Steve had even lived in the village of Peahi where Jaws was located without realizing its potential. His magazine, Maui Surfing, became the first media in the world to run a story and photos of Jaws.

In the late 1990s Steve composed some surf music and founded a surf music band. It was called THE WAVE SPIES. Steve became the lead singer. One of his songs got on FM radio on Maui, Australia and several stations across the United States. Several were aired on Maui television. In 2005, Steve sang a song called SURF RAGE which had the guitarist and composer of the "original" WIPEOUT on lead guitar. This song was aired on several television stations nationally and an impressive number of radio stations. In 2007 Omar's song SURFBOARD ROCK was aired on some TV stations with a surf video he directed. Merrell also played great guitar on this song and his Ocean Records produced this music. In 2007 Omar had these song videos on a popular Hollywood, celebrity, TV show for millions of viewers. Being a surf musician was the final phase of a long and memorable surfing career. In 2008 Steve moved to Central California and only rides a skateboard.

SEVEN

Unhappy And Happy Feelings

We experience a variety of emotions every day of our lives. Sometimes we feel unhappy. Other times we feel happy.

Why do we feel unhappy at certain times? A person may feel unhappy because he or she has not fulfilled their goals and desires. An unhappy person may feel unloved and rejected by other people. These unhappy individuals want something they aren't able to obtain. They desire experiences which cause them to wish for relationships that don't work out in their daily lives. So, these individuals feel unhappy and unfulfilled because they are not able to fulfill their dreams and desires.

Happiness is experienced when goals and desires are fulfilled on a regular basis. These individuals are respected, loved and honored by other people. They feel successful and fulfilled because they experience their fondest desires. Happy individuals are joyful, grateful and positive in their outlook about life. They tend to be achievers in school. They usually have a variety of friends they count on to share their values and beliefs.

Happy individuals generally maintain good health. They are happily married. These individuals are participating in activities they enjoy such as sports, music, reading, traveling, hiking, swimming, etc. They attend community events and generally are active in a variety of community activities.

Happy individuals inspire others to have hope, faith and awareness in God. They seek truth and wisdom which helps them to become truly aware and fulfilled.

Nonfiction

EIGHT

Daily Meditation

Daily meditation can help to bring peace and balance in one's life. Daily meditation is a time to evaluate one's life. Each moment of meditation can calm the mind. Each positive thought can uplift a person. Thoughts are creations.

Meditation is a special time when you can quiet your mind and awaken thoughts of higher consciousness to become one with your real self. Meditation is a time to look within in order to seek inner truths and to awaken to spiritual illumination.

Daily meditation can bring you closer to God. Meditation is a time to thank God for everything. Meditation helps us control our mind and emotions. We can raise our vibrations and begin our new day in a positive manner. Our lives can be improved because of daily meditation. We can learn to expand our consciousness and continue to awaken to truth and wisdom.

Some techniques to use while you are meditating are as follows. You can breathe deeply in timed and precise rhythms, hold your breath as long as you can and rapidly exhale. Focus only on your breathing with no other thoughts. Fill the deepest cavities of your lungs. If you perform vigorous exercise before this meditation you will be able to inhale deeper. Imagine all your energy concentrated in the Third Eye. This center is slightly above the eyebrows in the middle of the forehead. This exercise raises your cellular, mind and aura vibrations to a higher frequency of cosmic consciousness. You are also eliminating toxins buried deep in the lungs from air pollution, increasing the immune system and making the body alkaline to kill harmful bacteria and viruses. The healthier the body the more power is created to meditate. These breathing exercises are most effective outdoors in pure air in nature with negative ions. Avoid such breathing in indoor air, smog, vehicles and near fires. Polluted air lowers healthy vibrations and frequencies.

Next, chant certain words to become closer to the higher mind within the universal mind of God consciousness. One of the most powerful words is "Om" with the last letter hummed for a full breath. This word has a mystical vibration of higher frequencies of cosmic energy. Yogis and lamas in the Himalayas that have eliminated stress, disease and negative emotions, do deep breathing exercises before meditating and chanting. Om is a popular chant among the Buddhists. Metaphysical stores sell books with other chants which have several words. Major book store chains carry some of these books.

Focus on imagining a brilliant, white light which flows in the top of your body and down your spine into your chakras (centers with higher frequencies of energy and consciousness). Imagine the bright light filling your head, mind, throat, heart, navel and reproductive zones in steps. Picture this white light filling your entire aura surrounding your physical body. One goal is that no outside thoughts or mind pictures distract you from these visions. This accomplishment may take from weeks to years to accomplish. It depends on the frequency and power of focus. With sufficient practice and focus a person can actually _feel_ this white light filling all the cells, mind, chakras and brain with energy. The sensation of the white light will feel like a real substance.

The more minutes or hours this meditation can be continuously sustained the more potent the results. With proper application stress is eliminated, relaxation is attained, and bliss arrives with no need for drugs, intoxicating beverages or other artificial stimulants. Attention can be increased and physical energy is enhanced. Diseases are disintegrated by flooding these cells and organs with this white light and using it to vaporize and flush the viruses, negative bacteria and blockages out of the body. Mind power can push these diseases down to the bottom of the body and outside or disintegrate like a laser beam.

Each of the seven energy chakras in the invisible aura is meditated separately. The different chakras each have a different function regarding these different meditation goals. The proper chakra should be meditated upon. By properly meditating on all of these charkas at different times a Light Body Tune Up is accomplished. This technique balances and heals the physical, astral, emotional and etheric energy bodies in harmony. If all of these bodies resonate with each other at a perfect frequency matrix, excellent health, bliss, happiness and peace of mind result. Disease cannot enter this balance.

Temples and foundations like Yogananda Self Realization Fellowship, Astara, the Saint Germaine Foundation and meditation centers in many cities teach the many meditation techniques and chakra therapies.

Seek inner peace by focusing on God's Universal mind and awareness day by day. The more you meditate the more you can flow with the white light and love. Daily meditation can help you become One with God and all good.

NINE

Exercise Your Body

Physical exercise is important so we can keep our bodies healthier. Each day it is vital to walk a certain amount to limber our body muscles. Regular calisthenics should be used such as moving one's legs and arms back and forth, up and down and sideways. We should bend our body and do jumping movements.

Every exercise which is experienced each day may keep your body more fit and younger. Twenty minutes of daily exercise will help you feel stronger. Move your fingers and toes to keep them agile. Exercising fingers, toes and body joints can help you avoid getting arthritis.

Stretching, bending and spreading your arms and legs as well as hopping and jumping helps to strengthen your body. There are many muscles in the body as well as body tendons to exercise. Toxins can be eliminated in body joints and muscles by exercising regularly.

Exercising outdoors in the fresh air and breathing deeply to clean out your lungs clean out more toxins. Fresh air is important to breathe in order to maintain good health. Regular exercise helps us to maintain a better metabolism and we can burn more calories.

We may live much longer if we exercise on a regular basis. Our blood circulates much better when we exercise regularly. The more we walk the more we can strengthen our bodies.

So, keep on exercising to maintain your good health. You will be happier if you are healthy.

Nonfiction

TEN

The Cosmic Christ

The Cosmic Christ is the Divine Director who oversees all life. The Divine Director sends white light from the Central Sun in a higher spiritual plane in the Cosmos. The Cosmic Christ maintains the laws of Centralization, Love, Balance, Equilibrium, Unity and Harmony.

Beams of white light are sent out by the Cosmic Christ. The white light comes from the Great Central Sun to all living creations. The life force exists from God in every cell of each creation.

The law of Love and Centralization exists in every living creation. The nucleus is the central blueprint in each cell. The Cosmic Christ emanates light in the nucleus of each cell so the life energy may produce the creative function in each cell. The Cosmic Christ produces fohatic beings who have become creators of solar systems with a sun and planets around each star. Sons of Fohat are creators of living creations. They have created suns, planets, planetoids, moons, plants and the animal kingdom. The Cosmic Christ is within the Sons of Fohat.

The Cosmic Christ focuses on purity and the immaculate perfection in each life form. The Cosmic Christ is a perfect Cosmic force of Cosmic Intelligence and Creative energy which creates new creations.

We are affected by the Cosmic Christ which is the Divine Director of all life. We should become aware of the Cosmic Christ in our daily lives in order to awaken to divine truth and wisdom.

Nonfiction

ELEVEN

UFO Sightings Described In The Bible

There are descriptions in the King James version of THE BIBLE of UFO sightings. In Revelations Ezikiel described a four legs object that landed on Earth. He described a wheel within a wheel which appeared to be a spacecraft. Ezikiel went up in the wheel within a wheel. He never returned to Earth. This space vehicle appeared to be a chariot of fire.

Moses stated that he was led by celestial beings when he traveled across the desert. He stated in THE BIBLE that he heard voices speaking to him. These voices guided Moses across the desert to the Promised Land. Moses heard celestial beings talking to him on Mount Sinai. When Moses saw the burning bush he heard a voice speaking from the burning bush. It could have been a celestial being in a spacecraft blazing with radiant light in the burning bush who spoke to Moses. This celestial being advised Moses to write the Ten Commandments.

Enoch described a golden chariot in the Heavens in the Book of Enoch in THE BIBLE. This golden chariot traveled in the night sky blazing with light. A celestial being may have been in the golden chariot.

Lot described three beings dressed in white robes who suddenly appeared before him to warn him of a catastrophe where he lived. This experience was described in THE BIBLE. The three strangers disappeared as suddenly as they came. Lot was instructed to leave Sodom and Gomorrah with his family. Lot left this city. He was instructed not to look back. He was told he would turn to a pillar of salt if he looked back. His wife looked back and turned into a pillar of salt. Lot continued on his journey across the desert with his daughters away from Sodom and Gomorrah, which was destroyed. Some UFO researchers believe today that Sodom and Gomorrah was bombed by UFO spacecraft because the people had disobeyed God and had become sinners who could not be healed.

Nonfiction

TWELVE

The Theosophical Society

In 1875, Madame Helena Blavatsky, from Russia, came to New York City in America. She was contacted by Master Morya, who was her spiritual guru from India. Madame Blavatsky wrote THE SECRET DOCTRINE, which was a 750 page book about ancient wisdom awareness. Helena Blavatsky wrote ISIS UNVEILED, which was another esoteric book for the New Age.

Helena Blavatsky became the founder of THE THEOSOPHICAL SOCIETY in 1875. The co-founder was William Quan Judge. THE THEOSOPHICAL SOCIETY was the first metaphysical center formed in America. This movement spread to major cities in America such as New York City, San Francisco, Santa Barbara and Los Angeles in California.

Helena Blavatsky wrote KEYS TO THEOSOPHY which is about reincarnation and karma, known as cause and effect. Helena Blavatsky described in detail why we experience reimbodiment. She described the law of cause and effect known as karma. Followers developed a better understanding of occult principles and precepts of Metaphysics. More and more people came to THE THEOSOPHICAL MOVEMENT year by year.

Helena Blavatsky traveled to India to research rare and ancient wisdom and literature to develop Theosophy. Hindus already believed in reincarnation. Helena Blavatsky established an ashram in India. Indians were able to study Theosophy in India. They became familiar with THE

THEOSOPHICAL SOCIETY. Helena Blavatsky went to Ceylon near India and spread Theosophy. Madame Blavatsky based many of her writings on obscure, ancient writings in remote monasteries. These archives described lost continents like Lemuria and Atlantis, planetary cataclysms in ancient times, historical cycles, seven human root races, the evolution of humanity according to Divine Plan, great cosmic teachers and hierarchies, ascended masters, and thousands of years of lost histories of civilizations unknown to historians. The texts also detailed other dimensions or planes of existence and different types of cosmic beings and their purposes, etc.

Nonfiction

THIRTEEN

Wisdom Within

Wisdom within is acquired when we look within to seek truth. Truth is kept in our higher presence. The higher self is our Real Self. Our Real Self is our permanent self. The Real Self knows many truths and has recorded wisdom stored within it.

Wisdom within can be realized through meditation and right concentration. Right living helps souls to live by wisdom and light. Wisdom has existed in the Cosmic Plan for billions of years.

Souls who seek wisdom evolve into higher, Christ consciousness and service. Jesus looked within for wisdom. Gautama Buddha looked within for the truth and inner wisdom. He became enlightened and awakened because he looked within for wisdom. Mahatma Gandhi looked within for wisdom. He practiced nonviolence. He was a leader who helped to free his people in India so they could have independence from English domination. Gandhi lived a simple life of service and goodwill.

Jesus Christ had a deeper understanding of spiritual truths. He lived by the Golden Rule and brotherhood. He was aware of higher planes of existence and God consciousness. He awakened to wisdom at an early age. He served humanity and he healed many people.

Wisdom within our Akashic records can be realized when we meditate and focus on the inner voice of our higher self.

Nonfiction

FOURTEEN

World Government

World Government may be the answer for unity and prosperity of all nations. If wise leaders come together to promote one world government these leaders can promote world peace and prosperity to protect everyone.

A world constitution should be written. The world's citizens could band together to work for the good of all people in the world. World trade could be more effective. Employment of all eligible people could be established to benefit everyone.

Our world economy would be able to improve if one world currency is used. Humanity would be able to work for the common good of all of the world's people. Each nation could serve every nation to promote goodwill and brotherhood around the world.

World government can help world leaders work for the welfare and protection of all humanity on Earth. World currency can be used to pay for education, public services and transport of goods and services around the world.

Every world citizen would be able to promote prosperity and a better world environment to protect natural resources. War can be avoided because every country would cooperate with all other countries to serve the World government. The World government should promote freedom and peace for everyone.

A World government could promote democracy. Everyone could help chose political leaders because they would be allowed to vote. Freedom of speech should be allowed. Freedom of religion and occupations should be allowed.

Nonfiction

FIFTEEN

The Causes Of War

War is caused because of leaders who are selfish dictators who demand what they want without thinking of the needs and welfare of others. Dictators tend to be very aggressive and self centered. They tend to be war-mongers in order to control masses of people.

Reasons for war are selfish leaders who want natural resources from other countries such as oil. Oil is used in transportation vehicles. Some leaders own oil wells and oil derricks in the Middle East. They want to maintain control of their oil wells and derricks. So, these aggressive leaders start wars in order to stop Middle Easterners from taking over their oil claims. These selfish leaders haven't found peaceful ways to resolve their oil claims. They don't communicate effectively with people in the Middle East in order to protect their oil claims. Instead they cause wars unnecessarily.

Effective communication is the best way to overcome misunderstandings between certain political leaders who make wrong decisions which affect the safety and well being of millions of people. A group of leaders should research and study specific problems. These leaders should discuss every possible option to specific issues and problems. The best and most peaceful decisions should be made in order to avoid wars.

Unfortunately, underground conspirators cause wars. They make money from weapons and other war industries. It costs billions of dollars to send soldiers to war. Trillions of dollars are spent on futile wars caused by unwise decisions by unwise, political leaders who go along with conspirators.

Certain political ideologies conflict with democratic beliefs. Democracy should not be forced on people in other countries suddenly. People need to learn how to live by democratic principals step by step. In the Middle East such as Iran and Afghanistan the governments are not democracies. The political leaders like to do things their own way. The peoples' votes have little effect on who becomes the decision makers.

The Taliban are a militant group who are reacting to American soldiers fighting in the Middle East in order to promote democracy. The Taliban want Americans to leave the Middle East. They are killing many civilians while they are trying to fight against American soldiers. The Taliban feel that Americans shouldn't interfere in the Middle East especially with political philosophies. Unfortunately, history has shown that certain democracies have aggressively started some wars.

If Americans retreated from the Middle East the war would probably stop. However, the Taliban could theoretically take over and they would have a dominate hold on two countries in the Middle East. They would have control of oil in Afghanistan and possibly Pakistan. Americans in the West could develop more oil resources in America instead of depending on oil in the Middle East. However, this is not enough oil to make the United States self-sufficient and it pollutes the environment. Why not spend billions of dollars developing clean, non-polluting solar, wind and organic energy fuels? In Brazil sugarcane has replaced oil for fuel in a massive program. New Zealand has an excellent organic fuel program that has eliminated oil dependency.

Each country has a right to the kind of government each of them wish to establish. As long as certain countries are not threatening world peace these countries should be allowed to make their own decisions. War may be stopped if American leaders would withdraw from the Middle East.

Theory

SIXTEEN

The Star Of Bethlehem

THE BIBLE states that a star was shining over the stable where Jesus Christ was born approximately two thousand years ago. There are different theories about the star of Bethlehem.

One theory is that the star of Bethlehem may have been Jupiter in conjunction and alignment with Venus. Jupiter may have been moving in retrograde motion. This gaseous planet looked like a beaming star. Venus' light added to the brightness of Jupiter in the night sky because it was lined up with Jupiter.

The Wise men saw the star of Bethlehem hundreds of miles away. They traveled towards Bethlehem until they came to the stable where Jesus was lying in a manger dressed in swaddling clothes. The star of Bethlehem was beaming down over the place where Jesus was born.

Jupiter is the largest planet in our solar system. Jupiter appears very bright in the night sky. It looks like a star close to Earth because of its brightness. However, Jupiter is not a star. It is a gaseous planet. Jupiter is the first outer planet in our solar system.

People in Jesus' time two thousand years ago did not know much about astronomy. They were not familiar with the names and locations of the planets in our solar system. So, the Wise men thought Jupiter was a star.

Today, astronomers have traced the night sky to find out about the star of Bethlehem. Jupiter and Venus were the closest to appear in the night sky.

This astronomical phenomenon was unusual to the Wise men and people who saw the star over Bethlehem.

Another theory is the bright object which appeared over Bethlehem two thousand years ago may have been a flying saucer or UFO which hovered over Bethlehem beaming light down to the location where Jesus was born in a cave outside of Bethlehem. Is it possible that advanced, extraterrestrial beings were aware of the birth of Jesus near Bethlehem? It is more realistic that a bright moving object that moved across the desert and remained in one spot over Bethlehem was a UFO known as a spacecraft or flying saucer.

Different theories about the star of Bethlehem have been stated by scientists and astronomers. Two thousand years ago there were no telescopes and space cameras to study outer space. Therefore, people looked into the night sky only with their eyes. They were unable to use telescopes to observe stars, planets and moons in the night sky. We are yet to find out the truth about the star of Bethlehem.

SEVENTEEN

The True Mission Of Jesus Christ

The true mission of Jesus Christ is important to realize. THE BIBLE has the gospels of Peter, John, James, Philip, Mark, Thomas, Matthew, Timothy, and Luke. There were also the letters of St. Paul and Bartholmew. However, during the Middle Ages the scribes and priests of the Catholic Church destroyed some of the writings of the prophets. Some books of the Bible were censored out by directive of the Roman Emperor Justinian, at the Council of Nicea, in the 4th Century, A.D. Disciples of Jesus wrote gospels which were also tampered with and partially destroyed by priests and scribes and Popes during the Middle Ages.

Because the gospels written by Jesus' disciples were partially eliminated, his true mission was not revealed. For hundreds of centuries Jesus' teachings in their truest sense have not been revealed to humanity.

So, what did Jesus of Nazareth teach when he was on Earth? He spoke to his disciples and followers about their I AM PRESENCE. Yes, he stated, "The Father and I are One. What he meant is The I AM PRESENCE is the Father. The Father God is 18 inches above our heads. Within the I AM PRESENCE are spiral flames of white, gold, pink, green, violet and blue. White light shines in the center and beams out into the seven rays. All wisdom, knowledge, truth and divine intelligence exists in The I AM PRESENCE.

Jesus spoke to his followers about the Christ Self within each soul. He stated that souls who lived by Christ consciousness and who served their

I AM PRESENCE would be able to be healed of past karma known as cause and effect. The laws of love, centralization, forgiveness, polarities and cause and effect were mentioned by Jesus to his disciples.

Jesus was able to heal many souls who had faith. He lived by the will of God. He had only seven percent human karma affecting him. Jesus experienced soul mastery while he was on Earth. He lived by cosmic laws and he experienced Christ consciousness.

Jesus was known as Saint Esa in India. During the unrecorded 18 years of Jesus he traveled to India, Tibet and South America. He sat among Hindu priests and Buddhists monks to learn about their ancient religions. He was aware of reincarnation which means we reimbody again and again on Earth until we learn how to live by God's laws. Jesus was aware of karma, known as cause and effect. For every cause there is an effect.

The ancient Jews were aware of reincarnation. They knew they would reimbody again and again. Jesus spoke to the Jews about reincarnation. He mingled among the Essenes who were also Jews two thousand years ago. The Essenes were more advanced spiritually.

When Jesus sat among the Hindus in India he spoke to them about Christ consciousness. He told the Hindus not to worship false gods and statues. He spoke about the Golden Rule. He also prayed with Buddhists in the Himalayan Mountains. He knew about Buddha's Eightfold Path. Jesus agreed this eightfold path was the way to become enlightened.

Jesus Christ was a very enlightened, awakened person. He taught his disciples and followers to love God with all their hearts and minds. He focused on the Golden Rule and brotherhood. He realized that every thought, word and deed counts to develop and evolve on the path of overcoming the lower emotions and human habits and behavior.

Jesus was spiritually aware of the sacred chakras in the spiritual centers. Jesus was aware and in contact with the Great White Brotherhood. He communicated with Lords of Karma, with archangels, angels and Elohim. He was aware of the Great Central Sun and Heavenly Hosts. Jesus is a Lord who has served the Earth. He continues to serve our planet. He protects souls who call for his help and guidance.

EIGHTEEN

Chohans Of The Seven Rays

Chohan of the Seven Rays are Ascended Masters. The Seven Rays are White, Gold, Pink, Violet, Green, Blue and Purple-Gold.

El Morya is the Chohan of the First Ray which is the Blue Ray of God's will. Lord Lantos is the Chohan of the Second Ray which is the Gold Ray.

Paul the Venetian is the Chohan of the Third Ray which is the Pink Ray. Serapis Rey is the Chohan of the Fourth Ray which is the White Ray. Hilarion is the Chohan of the Fifth Ray known as the Green Ray.

Lady Master Nada is the Chohan of the Sixth Ray which is Purple-Gold. St. Germain is the Chohan of the Seventh Ray known as the Violet Ray.

Chohans are major leaders of given rays in the Great Central Sun. Lords of the Earth are Lord Buddha, Lord Jesus, Lord Shiva and Lord Maitreya. They oversee world conditions and help humanity as well.

The Chohans and Lords are important, spiritual beings who work in the Great Central Sun. They help to maintain peace, harmony, purity and balance on Earth and in the higher astral plane. They send out the white light and flames of freedom to protect all living things. They work with the archangels, angels, elementals and souls to sustain the Earth.

Nonfiction

NINETEEN

The Knights' Templar

The Knights Templar lived during the Middle Ages during the Christian Crusades. The Knights Templar formed their own temples. They defended Christianity and fought against anyone who tried to harm Christians.

The Knights Templar wore armor and carried weapons especially when they fought their enemies. They went to Israel to Jerusalem to protect Christians and to promote Christianity.

The Knights Templar were powerful over 200 years. They gathered treasures and gold and silver money which they kept in a secret place. The Knights Templar were prosperous. They established temples around Europe.

King Phillip had Knights Templar captured. They were taken to dungeons and treated cruelly. King Phillip had his soldiers search for the Knights Templar treasures and wealth. The king's soldiers never found the treasures and money.

The Knights Templar, who escaped, went to Scotland and other places in Europe to continue as Knights. The Knights who were captured and executed were accused of worshipping the devil and Satan. They were accused of heresy, etc.

The Knights Templar moved around Europe and Israel. They had a lot of influence on people in Europe for many years. They did not confide where their money and treasures were hidden. They lost their power once many Knights Templar were captured and killed. They will be remembered for what they accomplished and achieved.

The Knights Templar who survived also traveled to the New World to settle in North America at least one hundred years before Columbus discovered the West Indies. They may have taken treasures and money in their ships to the New World.

Nonfiction

TWENTY

The Philosophy Of Dolores Cannon

Dolores Cannon has focused on the field of hypnosis. She has traveled through time and space to explore the history of the past and the possibilities of the future. She has journeyed to unknown planets and dimensions and conversed with many so-called "alien" species. She has seen the wonders of lost civilizations and received information about their demise.

The only thing required is the use of the human mind. Everything known and unknown is hidden in the recesses of the subconscious where it awaits discovery. Dolores Cannon considers herself as the reporter, investigator and researcher of "lost knowledge."

Most of Dolores Cannon's work is hypnotherapy through past-life regressions. She said "her work deals with the unknown because she has discovered a method or technique of hypnosis whereby the realms of the mysterious and unexplored can be probed and examined."

Dolores Cannon said, "we are moving into a new world, a new dimension where information will be appreciated and applied. It was buried and lost, or held back for definite reasons. Many lost civilizations misused their powers and did not appreciate what they had accomplished, so the knowledge was taken away. It is time for these talents, powers and knowledge to come forth again and be appreciated and applied in our time period."

The main object of Dolores Cannon's work is therapy and helping people recover from or resolve their problems. The most exciting and thrilling part of her work is to discover history and to bring information and new theories back to our time. Dolores Cannon believes knowledge has been stored in the computer banks of the subconscious mind. It has only been waiting for the proper time to be brought forth once again.

Dolores Cannon has lectured all over the world. Her roots in hypnosis go back to the 1960s. She has been involved in this field over forty years. In the early days of her work she used the induction process which involved "watching the shiny object" where something is dangled or swung in front of the subject while the hypnotist proceeds with the induction. There are various tests performed to judge the depth of trance before the hypnotists could proceed. Some of these procedures are still used today and are still being taught.

Most hypnotists have progressed to much faster methods. Dolores Cannon developed her own technique by the process of elimination of the parts of the induction that were time-consuming and unnecessary. Modern techniques involve the use of the voice, imagery and visualization.

Dolores Cannon became involved with reincarnation and past-life regression in 1968. Dolores Cannon wrote a book entitled FIVE LIVES REMEMBERED. This book is about five different and distinct lifetimes to when a woman was created by God. All the sessions of this woman were recorded on a portable reel to reel tape recorder of those times. It was discovered that past-life memories were revealed which revealed why this woman was suffering from kidney problems.

Dolores Cannon found out that every physical symptom, disease or malady is a message from the subconscious. It is trying to tell us something and will persist until we finally understand. If we don't pay attention the disease or problem will continue to worsen until we have no alternative or until it is too late to reverse the situation. The same symptoms have related to the same problems in many people's present lives. Dolores Cannon wishes that the subconscious could find a less painful way to deliver the message. The subconscious thinks it is relaying the message in a direct, forward way that the person should understand, but this is often not the case. Dolores Cannon said, "We are too focused on our everyday lives to wonder why we have persistent backaches or headaches, etc."

Dolores Cannon believes that the subconscious is the record keeper, the equivalent to a gigantic computer. It records everything that has happened in the persons' life. If the person were asked to return to their twelfth birthday party they would be able to remember every event of that day, including the cake, those who attend, the presents, etc. The subconscious records every tiny detail. For instance, at any given moment you are being bombarded by thousands of bits of information, sight, sound, smells, sensory and much more. If you were to be consciously aware of all of this, you would be overwhelmed and unable to function. You must focus on only that information that is necessary for you to live your life

The subconscious not only records everything that has ever happened to the person in this lifetime, but everything that has ever happened to the person in their past lives and existences in the spirit state.

Dolores Cannon said, "I take the person to the lifetime that is most relevant or appropriate to the problems in their present lifetime. I never lead. I allow the subconscious to take the person to the life it considers to and the most important to view at the time of the session. I am always surprised whether the lifetime is boring or mundane (which 90% of them are), living in ancient or modern civilizations, or dealing with aliens and life on other planets or dimensions. The subconscious makes the connection and it is always one that I or the subject would never have consciously made. Yet it makes perfect sense when viewed from this perspective."

Dolores Cannon stated, "When I contact the subconscious, it always amazes me because it becomes obvious that I am not speaking to the client's personality, but a separate entity or portion of themselves. I can always tell when the subconscious is reached and answering the questions. It always speaks of the person in the third person (he, she). It is unemotional and seems to be removed or detached from the problems, almost as an objective observer."

Dolores Cannon said, "The subconscious pulls no punches, but tells the truth about the situation, as it sees it. When it has finished brow-beating the person in order to get the point across, it always tells them how much they are loved, and how proud they are of them for any advances they have made. This part also recognizes me, and often thanks me for putting the person into this trance state and allowing this process to occur. It often speaks of itself in the plural (we) as though it is not a single entity, but several."

Dolores Cannon has helped many individuals to overcome past traumas and negative memories stored in their subconscious. She had the most difficulty with "high-powered" businessmen and those who are judgmental and analytical. Instead of relaxing and going with the suggestions, they want to try to maintain control over the session. 90% of Dolores Cannon's clients have found a past life or more. Dolores Cannon has written 12 books about her findings, knowledge, investigations and research about unknown phenomena. These books from Ozark Mountain Publishing are highly recommended. Some titles are CONVOLUTED UNIVERSE Volumes 1-3, THE CUSTODIANS and KEEPERS OF THE GARDEN, etc.

Nonfiction

TWENTY-ONE

Jupiter, Our Second Sun

Jupiter is the largest planet in our solar system. Jupiter may become our second sun and provide heat and light to the solar system someday. Our sun may die out billions of years from now. Jupiter is a hot, gaseous planet which can become a sun.

The planets in our solar system may change their orbits and rotations when the sun burns out. The planets may rotate around Jupiter. Some of the planets may spin out of our solar system when the sun explodes and disintegrates. Some of the inner planets may explode and disintegrate when the sun dies and explodes.

Jupiter has always been gaseous and very hot. There are volcanic eruptions on Jupiter's surface. Very large flares of fiery flames can be seen on Jupiter. There are 63 moons which revolve around Jupiter. Europa is a moon which has water, is covered with ice and has possible microbes. Io is another large moon and the closet to Jupiter. Both moons are larger than Pluto. Ganymede is the biggest moon in the solar system.

Jupiter is the first of the outer planets. It is the fifth planet in our solar system. Jupiter is larger than the other planets put together. Jupiter sends out rays of light and heat into our solar system. As a possible, second sun in our solar system, Jupiter plays an important part. We should continue to observe Jupiter and find out all we can about it.

There are a lot of clouds on Jupiter which make this planet look like it has stripes. The clouds form bands of color which are blue, brown, yellow, white and red. The wind between the bands blows very fast. On Jupiter, winds blow as fast as 240 miles per hour. Jupiter's day is 10 Earth hours.

All the other planets in our solar system can fit inside Jupiter. 1,400 Earths can fit inside Jupiter. Jupiter has many storms. One storm is called the Great Red Spot. This storm is two times wider than our whole planet and like a hurricane on Earth. It has lasted more than 300 years.

Jupiter has more moons than any other planet in our solar system. Io has volcanoes and is about the same size as Earth's moons.

The space probe Galileo went to Jupiter. In 1994, pieces of a comet hit Jupiter. Galileo sent us pictures and then NASA crashed Galileo into Jupiter to avoid damaging Jupiter's moons.

Jupiter revolves around the sun in 4,331 Earth days. It is the fastest turning planet in our solar system.

TWENTY-TWO

UFO Underground Bases

UFO underground bases exist around the world where there are underground tunnels which lead to underground cities. These underground dwellings are inhabited by aliens and people on Earth. They are supplied with food, clothes and living quarters. These underground cities are lit up with electrical lighting and facilities. There is enough food in case of emergencies and disasters on the Earth's surface.

Some of the UFO underground bases are near Dulce in New Mexico, Area 51 in the Nevada desert and a remote, desert region in southern Utah. The largest of these settlements is a complete, underground city in Alaska under a forested valley. Pine Gap is an underground UFO base in the Outback in Australia. All of these underground bases are shelters with all necessary supplies and weapons.

UFO beings or aliens may be experimenting with animals and people they abduct to take under the Earth in some of the UFO underground bases. People in general are not aware of the underground bases and activities going on.

Some technicians, engineers and ex-military agents are revealing what they have seen in some of the UFO underground bases. Some wealthy people have gone underground in case of destruction on the Earth's surface. Some abducted individuals are forced to stay underground in cages.

Enough oxygen is being supplied underground so the people dwelling there can survive. The people living underground may be able to survive a holocaust if and when it takes place. Alien beings breed with human beings and live together. Aliens have learned to survive underground.

Nonfiction

TWENTY-THREE

Actions And Reactions

Life is made up of actions and reactions. Actions are causes and reactions are effects. Cause and effect means karma, which is a Sanscrit word from the East.

An action is Johnny is treated lovingly. The reaction is Johnny feels joy and love. Therefore, he is happy. Sherry was hit by a moving baseball on her head which was the action. As a result, Sherry experienced a concussion which was the reaction. Dick fell down. As a result of his fall Dick broke his leg. The action was the fall. The reaction was that he broke his leg.

Actions are what happen. Reactions are the result of the actions. The law of karma, known as cause and effect is an important law. All life experiences are actions and reactions. When birds move their wings to lift off the ground they begin to fly. The action is the moving of the birds' wings. The reaction is the birds are moving across the sky.

When a large rock is lifted this is the action. The reaction is that the large rock has been moved. When dancers move gracefully across the stage this is the action. The graceful movement across the stage affects the body and causes a reaction of bliss.

People who serve humanity are acting in the best interest of others. The reaction is that the people who are served benefit from this service which is the reaction.

TWENTY-FOUR

Florida's Stonehenge

In early 1998 when a 50 year old apartment building in the waterfront heart of downtown, Miami, Florida was raised up to be replaced by a new apartment complex a 38 foot diameter, perfect circle, which includes many post holes, cut-outs and basins, was discovered. James P. Grimes said this Florida Stonehenge site was cut into the limestone bedrock natural to the property. The excavation is continuing and has become a major archaeological find.

James P. Grimes said, "The site has proven to be a single massive structure carved directly into the limestone by some unknown people long before Ponce de Leon visited here in the early 1500s. The making of the circle had to have been a major undertaking, requiring knowledge of stone carving methods, proper tools and considerable manpower. It has 300-plus vertical post holes cut deeply into the stone on its surface and around its perimeter, plus a series of 20 well designed cavities or basins cut out across its surface. The rock was cut down to a depth of at least 4 feet around the circles exterior by its originators."

On-site investigation is being conducted by the Miami-Dade County Historical Preservation Division under Robert S. Carr. Excavators got off to a slow start because of funding and manpower constraints.

Some historical Indian artifacts have been found along with the skeletal remains of a 5 foot shark buried in one of the cavities. Census holds that the circle was carved about 2,000 years ago. Most investigators believe that the circle was built by the ancient Tequesta Indians, who inhabited much of southeastern Florida from 500 BC until they disappeared because of disease and wars in AD 1763.

Conventional guesses for the purpose of the Florida Stonehenge structure include an animal pen, a fort to guard the river entrance, a chief's house, a meeting place, or a celestial platform or calendar. Artifacts found include stone tools, shells, beads and broken pottery. Some of these could have been left by later inhabitants many years after the circle was built. Two basaltic, stone axes not manufactured in Florida are anomalous finds at the site.

Investigators of the 1950s and 1970s who knew and wrote about the Miami site believed, with Dr. Manson Valentine, that outsiders, not local Indians, created the circle.

Atlantean theorists have long argued that Miami is a site for the sacred temples of Atlantis. Florida was named Phaeacea during one of the Phonecian occupations when Loucathea-Tanith was the temple goddess. The Egyptians appeared to have been there earlier when the temple was dedicated to the god Min---which was the name Bimini.

The renowned British Atlantologist Edgerton Sykes, in his Atlantean Journal article "Atlantis in America" located the site exactly. "The Temple of Miami is now buried underneath the foundations of a hotel or office block. It has vanished on Bermuda. The Temple of Isis and Rephthys on Haiti still awaits rediscovery."

TWENTY-FIVE

Aztecs From Mexico

Ancient Aztecs lived in Mexico in what is known as Mexico City today. They built stone pyramids to worship their Aztec gods. Their Aztec temples were used for blood sacrifices. Many victims were stabbed to death at an altar at the top of the temples to appease the "gods."

The Aztecs used heavy slab stones which were tons of weight. How were the Aztecs able to lift heavy tons of large stones? Each stone was placed accurately on the stone below it. Each stone is tightly fitted. Aztec pyramids were well built. They were enormous and had an altar at the top of each pyramid.

Why did the ancient Aztecs perform human sacrifices? The Aztec priests believed that human sacrifices would please the gods and there would be enough rain and food for the Aztec people. The Aztecs experienced droughts and eventual starvation. Aztecs died from diseases.

The Aztecs worshipped the Sun. They chanted and danced in honor of the Sun and their other gods. The Aztecs planted corn, squash and beans. They sat in the Sun to enjoy the warmth of the Sun's rays,

The Aztecs were superstitious. They were able to carve stone images. Some stone images were their gods. The Aztecs developed symbols and numbers. However, they didn't have a written language which we can understand.

Hundreds of Aztecs eventually disappeared because of diseases and starvation. Jungles in Mexico have overgrown with vegetation. The pyramid, Aztec temples have been deserted because no ancient Aztecs exist there anymore.

Historians have investigated Aztec ruins and artifacts to learn about the ancient Aztecs.

TWENTY-SIX

Intelligent Beings From The Pleiades

Seven major stars in a constellation are about 500 light years away from Earth. These seven sister stars are called The Pleiades. Planets revolve around each of the seven, brilliant stars.

Pleiadians originally came from Lyra in another constellation to the Earth, which was a young planet rich in natural resources. Earth-Lyrans incorporated primate genetics into themselves. Other groups of Lyrans were on Earth to carry out the Founders' wishes by inserting Lyran genetics into the primates. "Desiring to build a new culture where they could become isolated from old conflicts rooted in their past, they explored the region widely before they decided on an open cluster of young, blue stars known as the Pleiades", stated Lyssa Royal and Keith Priest in their book THE PRISM OF LYRA.

The early Pleiadians (the previous Earth-Lyrans) possessed highly developed intuitive skills, as well as an inbred desire to create a community lifestyle, according to Lyssa Royal and Keith Priest. It took these beings centuries to mature and create their own identity separate from Lyran roots.

"Over centuries the community-oriented Pleiadians began to favor peace and tranquility. They learned to invalidate all forms of negativity," said Lyssa Royal and Keith Priest. It was proposed that a DNA transfer from the Pleiadians into the Earth Terran species over a long period of time would create a race of humanoids that would be terrestrial but would create a race of humanoids that would also have extraterrestrial roots. The closest ancestors of these Earth humans would be the Pleiadians. There were thousands of years of Pleiadian interaction with nearly every primitive culture upon the Earth.

Drawings of space beings and spacecraft adorn many cave walls and many ancient documents record the actions of these gods who came down from the sky. They saw themselves as "gods" no more than today's humans do. Some Pleiadians were light skinned, blonde haired, blue and purple eyed humans. Others were darker skinned, dark haired, dark eyed beings. Pleiadians were tall and slender. They wore white and purple robes and sandals. Many Pleiadians were spiritual beings who maintained a higher vibration and light. Some Pleiadians may have dwelled on Atlantis in ancient times. They were astronomers, architects, artists, priests, mathematicians and adept in metaphysics.

Pleiadians mingled among other races on Earth. Most Pleiadians traveled back to the Pleiades when there were wars on Earth. Other human root races have evolved on the Earth. However, the Pleiadians are a more spiritually advanced civilization. Their spiritual and adept awareness has affected the progress on Earth. Pleiadians still come to Earth to observe how Earth humans are doing. They are concerned about wars, starvation, and diseases on Earth. Pleiadians have communicated with some Earth humans as Billy Meier, etc.

TWENTY-SEVEN

Our Ancient Ancestors

Our ancient ancestors may have come from other planets in our galaxy. There are white, red, yellow, brown and black races on Earth. In very ancient times there were blue skin people. Ancient civilizations existed in Lemuria, Atlantis, Babylonia, Sumeria, the Euphrates and Africa. The Chinese (yellow races) existed in Asia. The brown races existed in India. The white races existed in Europe.

Ancient ancestors exist around the world in all major continents. We are descendants of ancient ancestors. Ancient languages have been preserved in scrolls, tablets and on stones carved into them. These ancient languages describe the beliefs and ancient customs and way of life of ancient ancestors.

Ancient religions have been recorded on scrolls, tablets and stones. Ancient temples depict statues of gods and venerated priests and other religious leaders. Some of our ancient ancestors have demonstrated religious ceremonies, chants and prayers. Ancient religious ceremonies have been carved out since early days. People worship the ancient beliefs that their ancient ancestors believed in.

Ancient ancestors chanted and sang ancient melodies. Their music described their religious beliefs and way of life. Their ancient dances have been learned again and again through century after century for thousands of years.

Artifacts from ancient ancestors have been found in ancient ruins and caves. Ancient drawings have been discovered in many cave dwellings. These ancient drawings describe animals, people and activities of ancient people.

We can learn from our ancient ancestors about religious beliefs, language, singing, dancing and art. We should respect and honor our ancient ancestors.

TWENTY-EIGHT

Flamenco Dancers

Flamenco dancing is a special style of dancing in Spain. Gypsies began Flamenco dancing hundreds of years ago.

The rhythm of Flamenco music is unusual and syncopated. Flamenco dancers move their feet and move around in a very creative, exotic manner with rhythmic, Spanish, Flamenco dance steps.

Flamenco dancers dress up in attractive, sensual costumes. Male dancers wear tight fitting pants and noticeable, dance boots. Tap steps are dramatic on a stage or platform. Flamenco dancers focus on very dramatic movements. Their goal is to entertain their audiences.

Female Flamenco dancers have a way of stimulating their audiences. Many Spanish ladies want to be Flamenco dancers. They idealize well known Flamenco dancers and they want to be able to perform the same way Flamenco dancers perform.

Flamenco dancers perform around Spain and around the world. Flamenco dancing is unique and unusual. Most people enjoy watching Flamenco dancing because of this unique style of dancing.

Fiction

TWENTY-NINE

The Golden City

High in the clouds above the surface of the Earth is a Golden City filled with light and pillars of beaming colors. The Golden City dazzles with radiant golden rays shining across this splendid city.

Golden temples existed in the Golden City. Golden streets glisten with shining light. The Golden City was magical and high in vibrations. Angelic beings with radiant auras and wings were flying around this Golden City. They were singing celestial melodies as they moved about freely.

The stars from the Heavens could be seen in the sky above. The stars sparkled with an effervescent glow. Violet, pink, green and gold colors emanated from the Heavens above this Golden City. Elohim and master beings walked along the golden streets and spiral staircases in this Golden City. Everyone magnified a heavenly glow and lived in harmony. They communicated with mental telepathy.

This Golden City moved around above the Earth. The Great Central Sun was nearby sending heavenly light into this Golden City. Celestial beings lived in harmony surrounded by blissful light. This Golden City had existed for eons of time. It is a blissful, joyful abode to behold. There are mystics who believe The Golden City is real in another dimension or parallel universe.

THIRTY

The Sacred Chalice

The sacred chalice was believed to be the cup Jesus passed around for his disciples to drink wine from. This sacred chalice has been missing after the last supper Jesus shared with his disciples.

Many people have searched for this sacred chalice. This sacred chalice was sacred because Jesus and his disciples used this chalice for a sacred purpose. It may have been a simple, silver cup.

The sacred chalice was thought to be in the Jewish Synagogue in Jerusalem in Israel. Some searchers thought the sacred chalice was in the ancient city of Petra in Jordan. Other people believed the sacred chalice was taken away by the Knights Templar of the Crusades.

No one is sure what happened to the sacred chalice. People are still searching for it. The sacred chalice is considered to be very valuable because Jesus drank from it. He stated that the wine his disciples drank represented Jesus' body. The bread and wine were symbolic and shared as a sacred blessing.

Jesus Christ sacrificed himself on the cross of crucifixion. He spoke the truth. He didn't compromise about the truth. He was accused falsely of heresy and blasphemy. Jesus said his kingdom is not of this world. Jesus was asked if he was the Messiah. Jesus replied that he came into this world to live by the Golden Rule and brotherhood. He came as a spiritual teacher to teach the truth to humanity.

The sacred chalice may carry the flames of freedom. It may have been charged with God's light and sacred energy.

Nonfiction

THIRTY-ONE

What Is Happening To Coral Sea Beds?

Coral Sea beds grow and spread in the ocean especially in tropical and subtropical zones. Corals continue to grow in clusters. They look like hardened flowers. They are pink, light orange and white. The Coral Sea beds are important in the ocean.

Fish and shell fish depend on the Coral Sea beds in order to receive nutrients. Fish and shell fish hide in Coral Sea beds for protection. Fish and shellfish are able to go under coral so larger fish cannot capture them for food.

Unfortunately, some Coral Sea beds are dying out in the Great Barrier Reef and Bermuda Triangle because of pollution drifting in the ocean. Pollution covers over Coral Sea beds causing them to stop growing. Coral rocks become discolored. They no longer provide food and nourishment for crustaceans and fish. As a result fish and crustaceans must go somewhere else for the nutrients they need. Some crustaceans and fish have been dying out because they no longer can depend on the nourishment and protection of growing, expanding Coral Sea beds.

Pollution needs to cleanse from the ocean toxic, harmful waste matter and poisonous chemicals. Harmful substances for warfare have been thrown into the ocean. These harmful substances plus other manmade waste matter drift in the ocean. This harms the plant and sea life as well as the Coral Sea beds in the ocean. In time, more Coral Sea beds will die out if pollution is not eradicated from the world's oceans.

Fiction

THIRTY-TWO

The Enormous Sea Turtle

The ebb tide splashed against the warm sandy shore near the Pelican Island in the South Seas. Clusters of coral, sea beds were spreading under the sea floor. Shell fish and tropical fish were moving quickly, darting in and out of coral caves and sea rocks. All was going as well as expected. Then, suddenly an enormous sea turtle emerged from the depths of the ocean floor to the surface of the ocean to take some deep breaths from the warm, tropical sea breezes. The enormous turtle remained afloat on the ocean's surface to look around. Barnacles and other crustaceans were clinging on the giant sea turtle's shell.

As the enormous sea turtle moved on the surface of the ocean it noticed whales spouting in the ocean. The whales flipped up and down with their swift, large tails in the ocean currents. The enormous sea turtle saw schools of dolphins swimming across the ocean. They rose up in the air and back down in the water.

The enormous sea turtle decided to follow the school of dolphins who were moving south in the direction of the South Pole. The dolphins kept swimming swiftly. The enormous sea turtle was able to keep up with the dolphins. The dolphins saw the enormous sea turtle moving towards them. They decided to dip down deep in the sea so the sea turtle would not see them anymore.

The enormous sea turtle went deep in the ocean in search of the school of dolphins. The dolphins went down to the ocean caverns to hide from the enormous sea turtle. The enormous sea turtle kept searching for the dolphins. He wasn't able to find them because they were hidden in sea caves.

A large octopus suddenly appeared with large tentacles. When the octopus saw the enormous sea turtle moving towards its direction the octopus squirted a black inky substance in the water. So, the ocean was covered with the black substance. The enormous sea turtle couldn't see the octopus anymore.

The enormous sea turtle wasn't able to see clearly in the ocean. So, it swam to the ocean's surface to look at the sky. Finally, the enormous sea turtle started moving north because it wanted to go back to its sea cave near the Pelican Island. The enormous sea turtle stopped along the way to swallow schools of smaller, tropical fish. The enormous sea turtle filled up with small crustaceans as well. It was full. So, the sea turtle swam with its large body across the ocean until it returned to its sea cave near Pelican Island. It was happy to be back where it was familiar with its surroundings.

Fiction

THIRTY-THREE

The Christmas Gift

Christmas is a special time of the year. It is a time to celebrate and to feast. Carolers sing a medley of Christmas carols as they go door to door. Christmas bells ring. Christmas cheer spreads everywhere.

Janine Thompson was the eldest daughter in a family of seven children. Her parents worked hard at manual jobs. Janine's father was a bricklayer. Her mother cleaned houses in the village where the Thompsons lived. The Thompsons were poor. However, they were sheltered and had just enough to eat. Jack Thompson managed to pay the annual taxes. Monthly bills were paid. There was little left after the monthly bills were paid.

Janine looked forward to Christmas every year. She enjoyed receiving gifts on Christmas Day. It was the best time of the year as far as she was concerned. Janine wanted to get her parents a Christmas gift. They had always remembered her by giving her nice yet simple gifts at Christmas time. She decided to make her parents a warm blanket.

Janine went to the yarn store to buy some colorful yarn. She had learned to knit from her mother. Janine began knitting a warm, woolen blanket for her parents' gift for Christmas. She began knitting the blanket in October so she would be done knitting it by December at Christmas time. The purple yarn was thick and beautiful.

The woolen blanket was half done by the end of November. Janine kept knitting until she finally finished the woolen blanket by December 20th. The purple blanket would fit her parents' double bed. Janine found some wrapping paper. She wrapped the homespun blanket in the wrapping paper. She made a home-made Christmas card for her parents. Janine put the Christmas gift under the Christmas tree for her parents. She waited for Christmas Day to arrive. She hoped her parents would appreciate her Christmas gift.

On Christmas Eve the Thomson family looked forward to a Christmas dinner of roast chicken, mashed potatoes, steamed string beans, buttered rolls, apple pie and apple cider. The Thompson family enjoyed sharing this delicious dinner. After dinner they sang Christmas carols around the upright piano. Janice played the piano while the family sang each Christmas carol.

The next morning the Thompson family got up and had a Christmas breakfast. After breakfast everyone went over to the Christmas tree in the living room. Christmas presents were under the decorated tree wrapped in Christmas paper. The Thompsons began opening their Christmas presents once Mr. Thompson handed out the presents one by one.

Janice waited for her parents to open her gift to them. Finally, after all the presents had been passed around to the Thompson family Janice's parents began opening their presents. Mrs. Thompson opened Janice's gift. She read the homemade Christmas card first. She smiled when she opened the card and read the message. Janice had written. "Merry Christmas and Happy New Year Mom and Dad. Thank you for being my parents. Much Love, Your daughter, Janice." Mrs. Thompson opened the present. When she saw the hand spun purple blanket she looked very pleased.

Janice's mother spoke to Janice. She said, "Janice, this is a beautiful blanket. Did you make it?" Janice smiled at her mother and replied, "Yes. I used woolen yarn and I knitted this blanket." Janice's mother said, "You made a very beautiful blanket! This blanket will keep your father and me warmer at night in bed. Thanks so much for this lovely Christmas gift."

Janice felt happy that her mother appreciated her Christmas gift. Her father saw the handmade blanket. He was very pleased that his daughter was so thoughtful because she had knitted a handmade blanket for her parents. Janice's parents felt this was the best Christmas gift they received that year. This was a very special Christmas for Janice's parents.

Cecelia Frances Page

Nonfiction

THIRTY-FOUR

Life On A Submarine

Navy men and Navy women live on submarines. Submarines are ships which go deep inside the ocean. The top of the submarine is sealed off so ocean water cannot come into the submarine.

Submarines must be supplied with oxygen when they are deep in the ocean. There are many chambers inside each submarine. The captain's chamber is where major instruments are located which are used to control the movement and speed of the submarine.

Staff and crew on submarines stay in specific chambers. Their living quarters are in a central location in the submarines. The captain and his crew must accept the boundaries of the submarines. There are narrow hallways and many chamber doors in each submarine. Chamber doors can be locked when necessary. Usually, chamber doors are unlocked so crewmen and crewwomen can move freely from one chamber to another.

Submarines have port holes which the captain and crew can look out of to see. The ocean and sea life can be seen by the captain and crew through the portholes.

There are chambers where crewmen and crewwomen can dress in underwater outfits. They are able to go out into the ocean with their underwater suits to move about in the ocean. Oceanographers study the oceans of the world. They may travel in submarines in order to go into the ocean to carefully observe and study the depths of the ocean floor and sea life which is not exposed to the Sun.

Submarines are valuable to navigate in deeper fathoms of the ocean.

Nonfiction

THIRTY-FIVE

Causes Of Global Warming

Global warming has been a problem in the world. Glaciers have been melting quickly. There used to be many glaciers. There are few glaciers left. Water is rising at the North Pole and South Pole. As ocean water rises flooding will continue to occur in Greenland, Iceland and North America and Canada.

Major continents could theoretically sink into the ocean in the future because of a lot of melting ice. Sinking continents are affecting the safety of people who build homes near the coast.

Global warming is caused by manmade pollution and heating methods. Heat comes out of gas and electrical stoves, clothes dryers, water heaters, smoke from chimneys, P.G.E. towers which send out smoke and heat and from the exhaust from cars, buses, trucks and trains. Heaters in homes send out heat. Factories produce smoke, gases and heat sent into the atmosphere.

The accumulated heat, smoke and gases affect the world's atmosphere. Icebergs are melting continuously because of the warmer climate.

Scientists, geologists and historians discovered that there have been cyclic, natural centuries of global warming. Some of these periods of warmer world climate were before the industrial age when there was not man-made, atmospheric heating. Skeptics believe present indications of global warming are cyclic rather than man-made.

How can we stop global warming? Manmade pollution and heating devices must be eliminated so the climate will not keep increasing the temperature around the world. Smokestacks and gases produced must be decreased enough to maintain icebergs. Icebergs need to be kept solid. The ocean will not continue to rise if the climate is cooler.

Everyone must avoid causing global warming by not over-using heating methods. Global warming will continue if prevention methods are not used. Everyone must make an effort to stop global warming.

THIRTY-SIX

Aggression Of The Taliban

The Taliban is a terrorist group which exists in Pakistan and Afghanistan. Taliban leaders and followers are causing war and death of civilians in Pakistan and Afghanistan. The Taliban is fighting American and British soldiers. They oppose democracy in the Middle East. The Taliban aggressors want to take control of the governments in Pakistan and Afghanistan.

The people of Pakistan must stay out of the streets and many public places during the days and nights. Cars and buildings have been bombed. Civilians in the streets have been shot and harmed. The Pakistan people are not safe.

Poverty and disease is a problem in Pakistan and Afghanistan. The Pakistan people have little say so in Pakistan. They want protection from American soldiers.

The government in Pakistan is not strong. Democracy does not exist in this country. In Afghanistan, democracy is being established. The people have been given the opportunity to vote. However, the Afghanistan government leaders are also dictating what they want to accomplish. This new government needs a lot of improvement.

American soldiers have been sent to Afghanistan to defend the new government there. American soldiers have been sent to Pakistan to stop their aggression and terrorism.

The war in the Middle East has been going on for eight years. It would be good if some compromises could be made so the war can stop. War is not the solution in Afghanistan and Pakistan.

A number of American troops are being transferred from Iraq to Afghanistan. A democracy has been established in Iraq. The people of Iraq are voting. The people of Iraq need to be restored and provided with clean water, enough food and better shelter. The Iraqis need more employment. Their economy needs to be restored. New buildings need to replace the buildings that have been destroyed.

The American government is trying to stop the Taliban aggressors from taking over in Middle Eastern countries. American leaders want the people in the Middle East to be free so they can make their own decisions. Some of the Middle Eastern people live by democratic values and beliefs.

Women in the Middle East need to be freed from abuse and dominate control from Middle Eastern men. Why should women in the Middle East have to wear veils? Why should they have to be escorted by fathers, brothers and husbands? Dictatorship exists in Pakistan and Yemen. Women in Afghanistan need to be freed as well. Iraqi women are still restricted by the Muslim religion.

It will take time for people in the Middle East to be free to change their lives. If they are able to vote and speak out about their needs it will help them to learn to defend themselves against Taliban aggressions.

THIRTY-SEVEN

The Need For Clean Water

Water has become polluted more and more in the world. Human waste and pollution has seeped into rivers, lakes, creeks and the oceans around the world.

We need to find ways to stop pollution from dripping into open waterways. Our waterways need to be protected so we can have cleaner water. Water is filtered and purified before it is used as tap water in our homes. However, extremely polluted water takes a lot longer to cleanse and purify before it can be used in our homes and public places.

People like to go swimming and surfing in lakes, lagoons, rivers and the ocean. They need to swim and surf in cleaner water. Suds and debris from pipes go out into the oceans. It is unhealthy to swallow unclean water in lakes, lagoons, rivers and oceans.

Chemicals are used to clean out unclean substances in water. Human waste matter and household debris should be sent under the ground through leach lines away from houses and public buildings. Suds and other waste matter should not be sent directly into oceans, lakes, lagoons and rivers. We must keep our waterways clean to maintain proper sanitation and good health.

We need water in order to live. Plants and animals also need clean water to remain healthy. Water is vital for our survival. We must have enough water to live. We cannot drink unsanitary, unclean water. We would become sick and come down with diseases if we consumed polluted water.

So, find ways to keep water clean and fit to drink every day. You will be healthier and you may live much longer because you have drunk clean water. Unfortunately many chemicals used to purify water supplies are toxic to plants and sea life. Chlorine and fluoride are toxic water purifiers in common usage. Distilled water and pure water from deep wells located far away from seeping pollution are preferable for drinking. Organic and biodegradable cleansers are preferable to chemical products. The healthiest water is done by osmosis machines which remove impurities and create high concentrations of oxygen and healthy, negative ions.

THIRTY-EIGHT

Political Propaganda

Political propaganda exists in the world. People listen to political issues and concerns on the television news and in different newspapers and magazines

Political candidates usually describe their accomplishments and achievements as well as their political beliefs and goals. Some politicians are Republicans. Other politicians are Democrats. There are politicians in the Liberal Party, Independent Party and Green Party. Each politician states his or her political beliefs and strategies.

Because politicians want to win in elections they find ways to slander their opponents. They say untrue comments at times about opponents to influence many people to vote for them instead of their opponents.

Stories are made up about candidates to stir up reactions. Political propaganda tactics are used to fool masses of people who are going to vote. Some politicians state what they plan to do if they are elected. After some politicians are elected they may not fulfill their political promises. They try to impress many people with strategies that they are unable to accomplish.

Some politicians have sincere reasons for going into politics. As a congressman or congresswoman, a senator, or a representative a politician can develop propositions and new bills to solve specific political issues and problems. You can write to the representative in your county or district. You can write to your state senators also about your political concerns.

Disregard false, political propaganda in the television news, newspapers and magazines. The Los Angeles Times, BBC American News and Wall Street Journal generally put out objective, true news.

Nonfiction

THIRTY-NINE

Progressive Methods Of Education

John Dewey developed progressive methods of education in the early 20th Century. He advised teachers to allow their students to participate in discussions, in groups and to learn to think and communicate effectively. He believed teachers should allow students to learn by doing. Teachers should not do all the talking. Students should be asked questions and be allowed to make comments.

Marie Montessori is another progressive educator who established the Montessori Method of hands on learning. She made tangible materials for Geography, Reading, Language, Mathematics and home graces. Marie Montessori placed tangible, learning materials on shelves so that children could select spontaneously what they were interested in learning. Marie Montessori discovered that children learn by doing. They are able to make decisions for themselves. They learn to think, recall and associate with the tangible materials they work with. Children are allowed to move around freely to pick and choose what they want to learn. Montessori instructors assist children individually and in small groups as they are learning to use tangible, learning materials.

Because the use of hands-on, learning materials, children learn faster and sooner about a variety of learning methods and subjects. They learn to read, write and participate in using tangible mathematical materials. They are able to develop social skills and to work independently as they are learning.

Children and adults can learn to work in groups. A leader and co-leader are selected to lead in committee work. Each member of the committee participates in gathering research and visual materials. The committees develop projects to present to audiences.

Computers are being used in computer labs and regular classrooms. Computer students learn to select computer programs so that they can learn all they can learn abut many subjects. Google is often selected because there are many options. Students are able to select Reading, Creative Writing, Mathematics and other academic subjects. They learn to solve word problems, multiple choice statements, fill-ins and matching items. The computer has become an effective, progressive way of educating many age groups.

Each progressive method of education has helped children and adults learn faster, better and more effectively. They are able to learn a lot more. Children and adults are much more motivated to learn because of progressive methods of education.

FORTY

Living In A Mountain Cabin

Living in a mountain cabin can be an interesting experience. Mountain cabins are built with pine or fir tree logs. Windows are made in each room. Curtains can be sewn and placed around each curtain.

Cabin floors are made of cut logs. The mountain cabin is generally designed with one large room which has a fireplace, dining room table and chairs and a living room area with a couch and wooden, log chairs.

Mountain cabins are built up in the high forest woods on mountain slopes and hillsides. The view is spectacular from the windows and outdoor surroundings. Beautiful, evergreen trees can be seen everywhere. Sometimes snow can be seen dripping onto the ground and tree limbs.

Wild animals such as deer, elk, rabbits, bears, foxes and squirrels can be seen from the front of and back of the mountain cabin as well as the sides of the cabin. The air is fresh and even crisp. You can enjoy the fragrance of pine, spruce and fir trees as you walk up mountain trails. This wholesome environment will uplift you. Being close to nature will help you feel good. God's nature creations are worth becoming one with.

The sounds of birds and wild animals can be heard in the mountains. Owls hoot. Mountain lions growl. Bears make loud, unusual sounds. Deer and elk scamper through the trees. Various birds chirp and chatter. Sounds in nature keep people alert especially when they are in a mountain cabin.

A mountain cabin is kept heated with burning logs in a fireplace. The warmth of the burning fire spreads around the mountain cabin. Food can be cooked in the fireplace on a metal holder. The cooking food smells delicious. Beds are put in corners or upstairs by climbing a ladder to a loft. Bedrooms may be near the sides of the cabin.

Mountain cabins can be very cozy especially at night. You can use candles and receive light from the fireplace as well. Mountain cabins are available near many mountains in the world. Switzerland is well known for mountain cabins because it is very mountainous. Austria is also known for its mountains. Mountain cabins are available near Austrian mountains.

In America mountain cabins exist near the Rocky Mountains, Mount Whitney, the Sierra Nevada Mountains and Mount Rainier. Mountain cabins make wonderful, vacation dwellings.

FORTY-ONE

Underground Shelters

Underground shelters have been built in many places in the world. Underground shelters have been built under major cities such as London, Paris, Rome, New York City, Chicago, Detroit, Los Angeles, San Diego and San Francisco, etc.

Underground shelters are carefully built deep under the ground. There are thick foundations to hold up the shelters. Tunnels built with thick cement blocks lead to the shelters. Electrical lighting has been established throughout underground shelters so that anyone who stays in an underground shelter will have enough light.

Underground shelters are supplied with necessary supplies such as food, bedding, blankets, bathroom facilities and places to sit down in order to be comfortable. The purpose for underground shelters is to protect many people in case of sudden bombings and holocausts. People will be able to go quickly into solidly built underground shelters so they can dwell safely from dangers on the surface of the Earth. They will be able to dwell for months in underground shelters as long as they have enough clean oxygen and food.

Nonfiction

FORTY-TWO

The Need For Electric Cars

With so much air pollution caused from gasoline and oil cars there is a need for alternative fuels such as the use of electricity in cars. The West, such as America and Europe, has depended on the use of oil from the Middle East. Oil is being used up rapidly in the world.

It would be wise to create more and more electric-cars. Electric cars can be built inexpensively with the use of electric charged batteries. More car manufacturers are producing electric powered cars. However, there needs to be places to recharge the electric batteries downtown. Perhaps electric batteries can be recharged at peoples' homes as well.

Alternative fuels are needed to replace gasoline and oil. We will not have to depend on oil from the Middle East if electric cars are produced from sugarcane and corn, etc.

Electric cars are much more economical because electric batteries can be recharged for pennies to the mile. Kramer and his volunteers who include engineers and electric vehicle enthusiasts, set out to raise awareness and funds to finance the development of a pure battery electric car and a gasoline-electric car hybrid.

J. William Moore, editor of Electric Vehicle World, an on line journal, promoted hybrid, electric vehicles. Electric cars can travel 60 miles an hour. William Alden developed the Starr car with a battery powered vehicle that he could drive from his home to an electric rail track. This 1960s invention was designed to attach to a narrow rail line that could be built to connect cities. The car would travel automatically at 60 miles per hour along these rails like a streetcar. Alden's prototype had a futuristic design.

The new Priuses is an electric car sold in Japan and Europe. It's that missing switch that may be the key to creating the first commercially available plug-in hybrid, what Calcars considers the "next generation" of hybrid vehicles.

The "Stealth Mode" is a car operated only on electric power with its IC (internal combustion engine turned off, operating much like a battery electric car. The driver runs an electric car for short distances up to one or two kilometers at less than 42 miles per hour.

Kramer noted that J.D. Powers and Associates reports that 35% of car buyers are interested in hybrid-electric cars and 85% of hybrid-electric car owners would pay more for these electric cars.

In late 2009 sleek cars powered only by electricity were manufactured and tested that could go up to 250 miles without being recharged. Some of these models could travel the maximum speed limits and accelerate as fast as most cars. Mass production was scheduled for 2011-2012. Some models are designed like classy sports cars while others have contemporary appearances similar to popular automobiles. Certain models can be recharged at homes and businesses with extension cords plugged into wall sockets. The main drawback is the costs are relatively expensive compared to many gasoline vehicles. Purchasing on monthly installment plans is a more affordable option. The new Tesla models are very highly acclaimed in the media.

FORTY-THREE

Cable Television

Cable television has come into existence within the last forty-five years around America and Europe. Cable lines are placed under the ground instead of on high-rise wired lines above houses.

Cable television offers many interesting and worthwhile channels. There are television programs about History, National Geographic, Science, Travel, Education, Art, Music, Dancing and dramatic presentations. Local, national and world news is presented every day so we can be informed of current issues, problems and social events.

Cable television provides a wide variety of topics and interests to select from. Before cable television existed people only received a few channels. The wide variety of channels with stimulating topics awakens viewers to more awareness about life. We are able to learn much more about many informative topics and issues.

Channels 8 and 19 are especially worthwhile to view. On Channel 19 there are excerpts of operas, operettas, plays, ballets as well as piano solos, vocal presentations, and a variety of dancing techniques and film exerpts. Channel 8 offers uninterrupted World News as well as special programs about nature, education and unique dramas.

Cable television makes a difference for many television viewers because of the many cultural presentations and variety of topics presented on a regular basis. We can appreciate the opportunity to select a variety of topics on different, cable, television programs.

Fiction

FORTY-FOUR

The Unfaithful Partner

When couples pledge and promise to be married they are expected to be faithful for life. They repeat marriage vows at an altar in front of ministers or priests and agree to look after each other even during times of illness and poor health. Couples are expected to be faithful to one another.

However, some marriage partners are not faithful to one another. One or both partners stray by having affairs with other people of the opposite sex or with someone of the same sex.

Max and Pamela Tyler were married in the First Christian Church in San Francisco, California. They had been married approximately ten years. They appeared to be happily married. Then, one day Max met another woman on a streetcar on his way home from work in San Francisco. This woman looked similar to his wife. She had brown hair, blue eyes and she dressed in attractive clothes. She looked about 32. Max was 35 years old. He was tall, lean with blonde hair and blue eyes. Max was attractive and sexually virile. He was attracted to this woman.

Max sat next to this woman on the streetcar. He decided to introduce himself to her. Max said, "Hi. My name is Max." The woman looked at him. She replied, "Hello. My name is Marilyn." Max asked, "Do you ride on the streetcar often?" Marilyn answered, "Yes. I work downtown. So, I take the streetcar to work five days a week." Max responded. "I work downtown five days a week, too."

Marilyn looked outside the streetcar window at the city buildings downtown. Max observed her closely. Marilyn sensed that Max was attracted to her. She noticed his blue eyes and blonde hair. She felt attracted to him as well. Max, asked, "What kind of work do you do?" Marilyn replied, "I am a business consultant for a firm downtown San Francisco." Max smiled at Marilyn. He replied, "I am a businessman downtown. I find it convenient to travel to work on streetcars. It is difficult to park a car downtown." Marilyn said, "This is why I take streetcars to work. It is also less expensive to travel by streetcar than by car."

Max remarked, "I work on Monday through Friday every week from 9 a.m. to 6 p.m. Perhaps we could meet to go home together." Marilyn responded. "I work from 9 a.m. to 6 p.m. I usually take the first streetcar available. I don't know you." Max answered, "Would you like to stop somewhere for a cup of coffee? Marilyn hesitated to answer at first. Max continued, "I would like to know you better. I know a place where we can stop to have some coffee."

Marilyn responded, "I am unable to stop to have coffee today. Maybe we can have coffee another time. Besides, I just met you." Max felt let down. He wanted to become more acquainted with Marilyn. He answered, "Can I have your phone number?" Marilyn replied, "Alright. My phone number is 774-3132. I live in San Francisco." Max quickly wrote down Marilyn's phone number. It was a local phone number because he lived in San Francisco, too. Max said, "Thanks. I will be calling you soon."

The streetcar suddenly stopped at the corner of Market St. and Ashbery Ave. Marilyn got up from her seat. She looked at Max with a smile. She said, "Nice talking to you. Goodbye." She walked to the streetcar door. The door opened. Marilyn stepped out of the streetcar. Then, the streetcar continued on Market Street. Max looked out of the window at Marilyn. She had walked onto Ashbery Ave to go home.

Max continued traveling in the streetcar through a long tunnel. The streetcar traveled on a streetcar track to West Portal Section. Max got off at 19th Avenue. He walked to a side street known as Maple Street. Max walked several blocks until he came to his house. When he walked into his home his wife, Pamela greeted him warmly. She said, "How was your day?" Max replied, "Alright."

Pamela poured some coffee in a cup and placed it near Max. Pamela brought Max's evening meal to the table. She had prepared meatloaf, mashed potatoes, mixed vegetables, rolls and butter. Pamela served another plate of food for herself. She also poured coffee in another cup for herself. She sat down near Max. They both began eating their dinner.

Pamela began talking to Max. She said, "I cleaned house most of the day. Aunt Margaret came over this afternoon for several hours to visit." Max was listening partially to Pamela. However, he kept thinking about Marilyn, who he had met on the streetcar. She didn't know he was married because he didn't tell her that he was married. He wasn't wearing a wedding ring when he met her.

After dinner, Max walked into the living room. He had finished his evening meal. He remained quiet during dinner. Pamela had no idea that her husband had met an attractive, younger woman on the streetcar. She washed the dishes and cleaned up the kitchen and dining room table. Max sat in his favorite chair and read the daily newspaper.

Max continued to think about Marilyn during the evening. He wanted to see her again. He had an opportunity when he was away from his wife, Pamela. That night Max tossed and turned because he couldn't sleep. He didn't make love to his wife. He didn't even kiss her goodnight.

The next day while Max was traveling on a streetcar to work he called Marilyn on his cell phone. Marilyn answered her cell phone because she gave Max her cell phone number. Marilyn said, "Hello." Max said, "This is Max. I met you yesterday. I would like to know you better. Can I meet you at the coffee shop downtown on Market Street today at Powell Street?" Marilyn replied, "O.K. I will meet you. What time do you want to meet?" Max answered, "Can you meet me at 6:30 p.m.?" Marilyn replied, "Yes. I'll meet you at the coffee shop at Market Street at Powell Street at 6:30 p.m." Max was delighted that Marilyn was willing to see him again.

After work that night, Max headed to the coffee shop at Market Street at Powell Street. He was anxious to see Marilyn again. He arrived at the coffee shop before Marilyn did. He waited patiently for her to arrive. Finally, Marilyn arrived at the coffee shop.

Max was sitting at a booth near the front window. Marilyn walked into the coffee shop. She saw Max sitting near the window. She walked over to him and said, "Hello." Max looked happy to see her. Max said, "Hi. Please sit down here." He pointed to a booth across from where he was sitting. Marilyn sat down where he pointed.

Max said, "I'm glad to see you. Would you like some coffee?" Marilyn said, "Sure. I'll have some coffee." Max beckoned a waitress. The waitress came over with coffee. She poured two cups of coffee. Max thanked her for serving coffee. Then the waitress asked if Max and Marilyn wanted anything else. Max asked Marilyn if she was hungry. Marilyn hadn't eaten dinner yet. She was hungry.

Marilyn said, "I haven't had dinner yet." Marilyn said, "The food at this coffee shop is good. Please order what you want." Marilyn asked, "What do you suggest I should order?" Max said, "Fish and chips with cole slaw is delicious." Marilyn decided to order this. The waitress wrote down her order. Max also ordered fish and chips with cole slaw.

Max looked at Marilyn with interest. "Tell me about your life. What are your interests and hobbies? What do you do during your spare time?" Marilyn said, "I like to play tennis, ping pong and chess. I read whenever I can. I like to read different books, magazines and newspapers. I like to go to the movies. I watch the History Channel, Science Channel, Education Channel, Travel Channel and Academy Winning dramas on cable television."

Max was fascinated with Marilyn's description of her hobbies and interests. Not only was she attractive; she seemed to be an interesting person. Max had become bored with his relationship with his wife, Pamela because she didn't show an interest in worthwhile hobbies and interests. This may be why he was willing to stray from his wife.

Marilyn asked, "What are your interests and hobbies?" Max replied, "I like to hike, play tennis and soccer. I also like to read and watch television. I also exercise and take sauna baths at a Men's Club." The waitress came back to the table with the two fish and chips dinners. The cole slaw was on the same plates. She also had a fish sauce for Marilyn and Max to dip their fish into.

Max stopped talking so he could eat his dinner. Marilyn was hungry. She was glad to eat this delicious dinner. While Max and Marilyn ate their dinners Max gazed at Marilyn. He was very attracted to her. He hoped she would go on seeing him after this first date. Marilyn was still attracted to Max. She assumed he was single because he wasn't wearing a wedding ring.

After Max and Marilyn had completed their dinners and coffee, Max offered to escort Marilyn to her home. They would take the streetcar. On the way to Marilyn's place Max talked about his job as a businessman. Marilyn talked about her job as a business consultant. Max and Marilyn were able to communicate effectively.

Once Marilyn and Max came to her dwelling place, Marilyn thanked Max for the date. Max said he wanted to see Marilyn again soon. Marilyn agreed to meet Max after work downtown on Friday night at another restaurant downtown on Powell Street. They met at a buffet diner.

Max and Marilyn became well acquainted after meeting regularly. Max would escort Marilyn each time to her apartment. He began kissing her and hugging her. Finally they were intimate. Max and Marilyn were passionate. Max revealed that Marilyn was very special. He told her that he loved her. Marilyn revealed to Max that she loved him as well. After months of relating intimately Max and Marilyn were inseparable.

Max didn't want to tell Marilyn that he was married. He had told his wife, Pamela that he had to work late at the office to complete some overdue work. So, Pamela didn't suspect that he was having an affair with someone else. After two years went by, Max finally told Marilyn that he was unhappily married. Marilyn was very disappointed that Max had concealed that he was married. She was very much in love with him.

Max decided to tell his wife, Pamela that he was seeing another woman. He had been unfaithful to his wife. Pamela broke down and cried. She told Max that she was pregnant. She didn't want to give him up especially when she was pregnant with his child. Max told Marilyn he wanted a divorce because he was in love with another woman.

Pamela tried to persuade Max to remain married to her. Max told Pamela that it wouldn't work out. He said he would give her money regularly to support their newborn child plus alimony money. Pamela was very upset. She had thought that she and Max would have a life time marriage. Max refused to give up Marilyn, who he had fallen deeply in love with.

FORTY-FIVE

Other Planets In Outer Space

Trillions of planets exist in our Universe. There are many solar systems in the Cosmos. Life exists on many planets. Life forms may be similar to life forms on Earth on other planets. However, many life forms are quite different on other planets in outer space.

Temperatures are extremely hot as well as extremely cold. Each planet in outer space is affected by the sun they revolve around. If the sun is much larger than our sun it may give out more heat and light. The planets moving around larger suns are probably much larger planets than we have in our solar system.

The largest planet in our solar system is Jupiter. Jupiter is a gaseous planet. It is at least 3,000 degrees. Life, as we know it, doesn't exist on Jupiter. Other planets in outer space are like Jupiter. They are large, very hot and gaseous.

Planets in outer space may be very similar in size as the Earth. Oceans, planets and animals exist on other planets in outer space. Human beings also exist on many planets in other solar systems.

Human beings on Earth originally came from outer space in the Pleiades, Orion, Sirius, ancient Mars and other realms in outer space. The book entitled EXTRATERRESTRIAL CIVILIZATIONS ON EARTH written by Steve Omar and Cecelia Frances Page has evidence about extraterrestrial human-like beings that traveled to Earth in ancient times, who inhabited different continents on Earth. Billy Mier was contacted by extraterrestrials that came to Earth in their spaceships. They communicated with Billy Mier.

Other individuals such as Eric Von Daniken, Zecharia Sitchin, David Childress and Bill Birnes have gathered evidence about extraterrestrials who have traveled to Earth. Eric Von Daniken gathered tangible evidence such as cave drawings, carvings on rocks, statuettes, ancient writings and paintings.

The Cosmos continues to expand and grow. Earth is only one of millions of planets in our Universe. Life exists everywhere in our Universe. Highly intelligent beings exist on other planets in outer space. We need to be open-minded about intelligent life which exists in the Universe.

Life also exists on different dimensions. Inner dimensions are invisible to us. Higher vibrations and light exist on inner dimensions. Other planets exist in parallel dimensions.

FORTY-SIX

Significant Visions

Significant visions have awakened different individuals to higher awareness. Jesus Christ, Gautama Buddha, Moses, Krishna, Yogananda and others have had significant visions. They were able to experience visions of inner planes and dimensions.

Jesus Christ was able to see the Kingdom of Heaven. He communicated with Elohim, other Masters, archangels and angels who he was able to envision in his inner eye. Gautama Buddha meditated regularly under a Bo tree. He was able to experience Nirvana, a heavenly, blissful place in the inner kingdom. He experienced illumination and pure light. He was inspired and uplifted by his inner experiences.

Moses, an ancient Israelite leader, saw visions about the promised land. He saw visions of a burning bush. He led the Israelite people out of Egypt to Israel where they established the promised land. The Jewish religion flourished in Israel. Moses listened to a voice within his inner mind.

Yogananda awakened to the energy of God within his sacred chakras. He had visions of higher realms. He centered on his spiritual, inner eye. He was able to experience peace, harmony and serenity. He was guided by his inner visions.

Souls seeking illumination and enlightenment can experience unusual, extrasensory visions of inner dimensions. There are heavenly abodes in the invisible dimensions or inner planes. Heavenly beings can appear before those who can see with their inner eye. These heavenly beings radiate with light. They wear robes of light. Their auras expand out and are visible to awakened souls.

Nonfiction

FORTY-SEVEN

Conspiracies In The World

Conspiracies exist around the world. Why are there conspiracies? People who are extremely wealthy, who are part of large, underground movements, become involved with making more money. They make a lot of money by selling warfare weapons, by selling harmful drugs and producing factories which cause a lot of pollution in the environment.

Conspirators help cause unnecessary wars. Many innocent people have been killed because of wars. More civilians have been killed than soldiers. Secret conspirators influence major leaders in the world. They like to control world leaders so they can be powerful. Their goal is to control the world.

Conspiracies exist in different governments. It is difficult to achieve certain necessary goals such as promoting enough employment, food and shelter for unemployed people as well as homeless people. Too much money is spent on wars. Tax money used for unnecessary wars should be used to help people in need of food, shelter and education.

Conspirators do not live by the Golden Rule. They conspire to cause harm and destruction on Earth. They go around secretly causing serious economic and environmental problems in the world. Conspirators are not concerned about the welfare and safety of others. Their desire is to accumulate wealth and power for themselves.

Conspirators misuse funds at banks, businesses and in governmental institutions. They tend to steal money wherever they can receive it. When big bankers were given a big hand out by the American government to save their banks from bankruptcy they gave out unfair bonuses to bankers who were undeserving. The government money came from American taxes. As a result, Americans have suffered because the misused money could have been used to promote employment as well as be used to provide food and shelter for needy people.

Conspirators think about what they want for themselves at the expense of other people. Conspirators are very selfish and self centered. Conspirators go against the desires and needs of many people. They slow progress down because of their negative ways and harmful actions.

FORTY-EIGHT

Life At A Lagoon

Life at a lagoon can amaze us. Serene, placid water appears like clear blue mirrors to viewers. The sun dazzles and reflects in a lagoon. Sunlight flickers in the water. As the sun rises in the sky geese, ducks, seagulls, moorhens and sparrows move towards the lagoon.

Geese swim in a line gracefully across the lagoon and step out on embankments to nipple more grass and hidden seeds in the grass. Ducks waddle onto the grassy inclines. They nibble grass and seeds. After grazing on the grass the geese clean their feathers and then sit down on the grass to rest and take a nap.

Many moorhens gather together to nipple grass and swallow seeds. They stay close together. Then they go into the lagoon to swim and wade around. They bob their heads into the lagoon looking for bugs.

Suddenly, some people arrived at the lagoon with food. The geese, ducks, moorhens and seagulls swiftly gather near the people waiting for bits of food thrown to them. They swallow the scraps of food quickly. They are eager for more scraps of food to be thrown to them.

As soon as all the food has been thrown or handed carefully to the eager lagoon birds, they go on eating grass and seeds. Geese become very excited when people arrive to feed them. They expect to be fed scraps of food. They appear disappointed because there are no more scraps of food.

Seagulls fly in flocks over the lagoon hovering over the water to scoop down to the lagoon for food. Many of the seagulls land in the water and float around near each other. Some seagulls make loud sounds as they call to each other.

When the sun moves closer to the Western horizon sunset colors of orange, red, yellow and purple reflect in the lagoon creating a colorful array of designs. Then it becomes darker. Street lamps and house lights reflect in the lagoon during the night.

The moon may come out and reflect in the lagoon. A full moon lights up the night sky. The shape of the moon can be seen in the lagoon.

The geese, seagulls, moorhens and sparrows leave the lagoon and return to their nests in reeds and trees. Geese usually dwell in reeds near a lagoon. Ducks may also dwell in reeds near a lagoon. Moorhens usually fly away and go back to their nests.

The next day geese, ducks, moorhens and sparrows come back to the lagoon. They continue to glide in the lagoon. They nibble grass and seeds again. They rest while they sun themselves when they are done eating. Lagoon birds repeat this pattern every day and night.

FORTY-NINE

Excerpts On Channel 19

Channel 19 is a local educational channel known as COETV. Dr. Julian Crocker, Superintendent of San Luis Obispo County, is the narrator and host to COETV. He focuses on educational programs.

Generally from 9 p.m. to 8 a.m. special excerpts such as ballet, vocal solos, piano solos, orchestra selections and modern dances as well as dramatic episodes are presented on COETV on Channel 19 on Charter television.

Frederic Chopin's piano concerto in C Minor, and his Mazurkas and Polonaises have been presented by Van Cliborn and Victor Borge. Claude Debussy's piano pieces have been presented at Carnegie Hall and Schubert Hall. Liberace has presented a variety of classical and semi-classical piano solos such as the <u>Moonlight Sonata</u> and <u>Largo</u> at New York Entertainment Center. Horiwitz, who was still performing at 97, played Edward Grieg's piano solos.

Many ballet excerpts such as the <u>Nutcracker Suite</u> and <u>Swan Lake</u> as well as many other ballet performances are viewed. <u>La Boheme</u> is a very famous opera composed by Puccini in Italy. This famous opera has been filmed and presented on COETV on Channel 19. Excerpts of <u>Maytime</u>, <u>My Fair Lady</u>, <u>Brigadoon, Westside Story, Oklahoma</u> and other well known musicals have been presented on COETV on Channel 19.

Vocal soloists such as Marian Anderson, Leotine Price, Dinah Shore, Judy Garland, Kathryn Grayson, Beverly Sills and others perform vocal solos on COETV on Channel 19.

These excerpts are worth viewing on COETV on Channel 19.

FIFTY

Take Care Of Your Teeth

It is important to take care of your teeth. Without teeth we would have to depend on false teeth in order to chew our food. Healthy gums are necessary for maintenance of a healthier body.

Our teeth should be brushed carefully after every meal. Use a wooden toothpick to clean between each tooth. Use a special holder to apply the point of a wooden toothpick to clean in the upper and lower gums for each tooth. Plaque can build up on the porcelain of our teeth if they are not properly and carefully brushed.

Dental floss is used often to clean between one's teeth. Dental floss removes plaque between our teeth. Rinse your gums and mouth after washing your teeth. Your teeth will look much whiter if you use an effective toothpaste and tooth whitener to polish your teeth.

Healthy, clean teeth look attractive when we smile. The whiter our teeth look the better we look in general. We should see a dentist at least every six months for a regular check up. X-rays should be taken at least every two years to check for cavities and bone loss.

To keep one's teeth cleaner a person should have his or her teeth cleaned by a teeth cleaner specialist. Your teeth will be cleaner and remain healthier if they are cleaned at least every four months.

Colgate and Crest toothpastes are recommended to use for brushing your teeth. These toothpastes help to prevent cavities in your teeth. So, keep care of your teeth by washing them and having them checked by a dentist and hygiene specialist. Healthier teeth will help you have healthier gums. You will be healthier.

FIFTY-ONE

Seafood Dishes

There is usually an abundance of fish and shellfish in the ocean. Fishermen fish for large quantities of fish and shellfish in the ocean as well as in major lakes and rivers.

Many restaurants in the world serve fish and shellfish as seafood dishes. Customers order salmon, tuna, sole, cod, red snapper, shrimp, calamari, lobsters, abalones, crabs, trout, shark, silver fish, sea bass, flounder, squid, octopi and more sea food.

There is a wide variety of seafood dishes to choose from at seafood restaurants. Generally rice, French fries, baked potatoes, potato scallops, macaroni and cheese, hash browns, and country fried potatoes with sautéed onions and green pepper are served with seafood. Mixed vegetables, green salads and chopped, cut, raw vegetables can be served with seafood dishes. Seafood can be baked, fried or steamed.

FIFTY-TWO

How Modern Conveniences Affect Us

In earlier times there were no modern household conveniences. All chores had to be done by hand and physical labor. Clothes were washed in nearby streams by hand and on wash boards. Wood was cut to burn in a pot belly stove. Food was cooked in fireplaces as well by pioneers in America. Livestock and chickens were cared for. Eggs were collected in chicken pens. All food was prepared from scratch. Fireplaces were used in every home over one hundred years ago. People were used to doing all of the work. They worked long hours to provide for themselves.

Clothes were hand made. Women knitted stockings, blankets, scarves, shawls and hand cloths. They sewed dresses, pants, shirts, coats, blouses, skirts and knitted sweaters, etc. Floors were washed and swept by hand. People were used to working hard. They worked many hours at least six days a week. On Sundays most people went to church and also spent time with their families.

Many people today enjoy far more leisure time because they finish their housework quickly. They are able to shop in grocery stores for what they need. There are many available frozen foods, canned goods, cut meats and fish, pastries and delicatessen specialties. Dairy products such as milk, cheese, cottage cheese, icecream, yogurt, a variety of juices, tea and coffee as well as hot chocolate are available.

Modern generations have many modern conveniences so they are able to relax and have more time to do what they want to do. Some people watch television and listen to the radio. They use DVD players and cassettes. Cell phones are used by millions of people. People can communicate readily with other people.

In the early days people traveled by wagons, horses, stage coaches, mules and go-carts. It took a lot longer to travel to their destinations. Today people travel quickly by cars, trucks, vans, trains, airplanes and even by motorcycles to their destinations. They arrive a lot sooner to where they want to go. Today's transportation makes it much easier to go many places quickly.

People tend to be lazier today because they don't have to work so hard to survive. However, many people work at least 30 to 40 hours a week at their jobs in order to earn a living. They have bills to pay each month for a house or to rent a house or apartment plus all utilities. They need to pay for their groceries and transportation. Miscellaneous items need to be paid for regularly.

People are able to take more vacations as long as they have saved enough money to pay for them. They are able to travel long distances to many different places. People can travel by Amtrak, airplane, cruise ships, cars and RV vans. People are able to enjoy leisure time more today because of the use of modern appliances.

Nonfiction

FIFTY-THREE

Old Fashion Customs

Old fashioned customs still exist in the minds of elderly people. For instance, men used to open the car door for women. The custom has been for a newly-wed husband to carry his bride over the threshold of their new home. The bride wears something new and something old as well as something borrowed. The tradition is to be married in church. A wedding reception is given after the wedding. Married couples still exchange wedding rings which are made of gold or silver.

Other, old fashion customs are to set knives, forks and spoons on the dinner table. Napkins are used at the dinner table. Food is served at the dinner table. The custom is to wait until the food is served before everyone eats. Generally a prayer is repeated before the meal is started.

An old fashion custom is to say please, thank you, you are welcome, hello and goodbye as common courtesies. Elderly people are helped across the street.

Usually, elderly people are treated with more respect because of their age. Elderly people recall being silent at the table. They were obedient because they accepted old fashion values.

It is an old fashion custom to bow after performing on the stage. Flowers are given to performers to honor them after their performances.

In the West, women generally walk in front of men. In Asia and India, women still walk behind their husbands, fathers and brothers. Many people worship God and attend church.

Old fashion customs still exist. Some old fashion customs are no longer acknowledged. We do not kneel before our spouse. Men made all or most of the decisions in the past. Now, women are making more and more important decisions in their marriages and their family life. Women were not treated as equals to men in the past. Today, more and more women are being treated as equals to men.

Old fashion customs continue in the Middle East. Moslem women are required to wear veils. Women must be escorted by men in public places. Women are treated subservient to men. However, some women in parts of the Middle East are becoming more educated. These women don't wear veils. They may acquire good jobs. These women are becoming more liberated step by step. Some women are given the opportunity to vote. Some women are not escorted in public. Some women in the Middle East are free to speak.

Some old fashion customs are worth preserving while other old fashion customs should be discontinued. A man usually is the leader when a couple dance. Vocal soloists generally are expected to stand up front facing their audience. Well known orchestra directors and participants in the orchestra are expected to dress up in formal attire to perform before audiences. Opera performers dress in costumes to perform on stages. It is the custom to dress up before performing for audiences.

A gentleman helps a lady to be seated when he takes her out to eat at a restaurant or café. He walks beside her in the street when they go somewhere. It is a custom to answer the door when someone comes to visit.

FIFTY-FOUR

How Scammers Fool People

Scammers are individuals and groups of people who pretend to have millions of dollars to give away. They advertise on the internet. Their main purpose is to fool as many people as they can by telling them that large sums of money will be wired or mailed or delivered to their victims after fees are paid.

Innocent, ignorant people may be fooled by scammers. Scammers continue to ask their victims for money. Once a person sends the scammer some money, then the scammer asks for more money. They start by saying a fee must be paid. Then taxes must be paid. Then bank costs are incurred. Then the scammer says the money can't be transferred because the deliverer has been in a car accident or the deliverer died.

Meanwhile, the victim has already paid $2,500 or more to the scammer. The scammer keeps making excuses for not sending the promised money. Then a check for the promised amount is either mailed or delivered at the victim's door.

So, the victim takes the check to the bank to deposit it in his or her savings account. The bank teller takes the check to the back room at the bank to check to find out if it is a valid check. The bank teller brings the check back to the customer. He or she says, "This check can not be cashed and deposited in your savings account because this check is not valid." So, the customer finally finds out that the so called money sent by a check is a hoax! He or she has spent $2,500 that has been lost! He or she will not be able to get the $2,500 back.

Scammers tempt elderly people who are desperate for large sums of money. Elderly people may be vulnerable and trusting of scammers.

Some individuals trust different scammers. Scammers lie and state that they are bank officials, government workers and pretend to be Bill Gates, who is a very wealthy person. Ignorant, vulnerable people read about different scams on the internet.

Scammers continue to call their victims over and over to collect more money. They call very late at night and very early in the morning to persuade their victims to send more money. Scammers don't have large sums of money to give away. Instead, they gather up all the money they can to acquire wealth. Scammers depend on other peoples' money to survive.

Many scammers advertise on the internet in newspapers and some magazines. They ask people to contact them by a phony e-mail address. Scammers write e-mail letters to their customers, who fall for their lies and pay their fees.

Gullible individuals may spend their life savings because they believe they will eventually receive millions of dollars. Each scammer continues to fool vulnerable people who refuse to see through scammers strategies to fool them. These gullible individuals end up with very little money to live on. They refuse to listen to warnings about scammers schemes.

Many scammers exist in Africa, especially in Nigeria, Kenya and South Africa. Scammers exist all over the world such as America, England and Holland, etc. They generally use false identification so they can't be traced. Scammers use false seals and certificates as well as false titles to fool others.

Bankers have been fooled at times by false checks. Money has been stolen from big banks. The victims who cash scammers false checks must pay the bank back. Many banks have become aware of scammers especially from Nigeria, England, America and Holland. Banks have become very cautious about phony checks from scammers. So, be aware of scammers who try to fool you!

FIFTY-FIVE

Morality Versus Immorality

Morality means that society lives by specific moral expectations. Moral values and codes are developed for many people to live by.

Some morals are as follows. People are not allowed to steal from others. People are expected to tell the truth. Lying is considered immoral conduct. Moral values include how we treat others with fairness and decency.

Men and women who don't have sex until they have a meaningful and loving relationship are maintaining moral standards. Men and women who are not promiscuous and are able to be true and faithful are considered to be moral. Unfaithful spouses are labeled as immoral.

Individuals who express self responsibility and maintain jobs to pay their bills are considered to be moral. People who keep losing their jobs are considered irresponsible and even lacking in proper conduct.

Individuals who are vulgar and use profane language are considered to be immoral. Individuals who think immoral thoughts are being immoral in their consciousness. Students who deliberately misbehave in classrooms at school are immoral because of misconduct.

Drug dealers and drug takers are immoral because they are destroying other people's lives as well as their own lives. LSD, coke and other drugs are very harmful to take. Drug takers become mentally imbalanced. They become mentally ill. It is immoral to take harmful drugs that derange one's mind.

Immoral conduct causes individuals to break moral laws. Responsible, law abiding individuals are moral. They protect themselves and others by obeying manmade laws and God's laws.

Fiction

FIFTY-SIX

Why People Gossip

Why do people gossip? What is gossip? Gossip means a person speaks unnecessarily, critically and even falsely about other people. A person who has the habit of gossiping is someone who does not focus on the higher self or real self within. This individual feels frustrated, hateful, jealous, resentful and possibly incomplete. Because of lower emotions taking over, a person develops the habit of gossiping about others in order to feel the empty void in their lower mind.

Sally Jones worked as a stenographer in a large business firm in Chicago, Illinois. She had been working there for approximately three years. Sally became familiar with other office workers. She went to coffee break for twenty minutes in the mid morning and mid afternoon. Often, she heard office employees gossiping about their relationships with other people they associated with. She heard Sue gossip about her husband in a derogative manner. Sue spoke to several office associates who were sitting near her. Sue said, "My husband Billy is so lazy at home! He won't help me around the house. He refuses even to empty the garbage! He also refuses to watch our children when I have to go shopping for groceries!" Mary Jean, who was sitting nearby, responded by saying, "I know how you feel! My husband refuses to help me with the dishes after we are done with our evening meal. In fact, he refuses to empty the garbage. He walks our dogs. But, he doesn't clean up after them when they mess up the floors in our house! I do all the cooking, cleaning, shopping and bookkeeping! I am fed up!" Sue replied,

"I guess I am not the only one with a husband who refuses to help around the house!" Rachel, who was sitting nearby, listened intently to Sue and Mary Jean. She remarked, "I'm not married. I don't even have a boyfriend. I have to do everything for myself. I haven't met someone yet who I want to get serious about. Maybe I am better off being on my own!"

It was time to go back to work in the office. The twenty minutes was up. Everyone had their mid morning break. Sue, Mary Jean and Rachel as well as other office workers went back to their office to continue working. They continued doing stenographer assignments.

At lunchtime, most of the office employees stepped out of the office to go to lunch for an hour. Some of them went into the employee lounge room to eat their sack or box lunches of sandwiches, fruit and hot or cold drinks. Some of the employees bought canned sodas from a soda machine to drink.

Sue and Rachel stepped out of the office to eat in a nearby café downtown Chicago. Once they entered the café they sat at a booth. They ordered fish and chips and clam chowder. Sue replied, "My husband refuses to let me go anywhere without him. I think I am going to tell him that I need to go see my parents who live in Baltimore, Maryland. If he doesn't want to go, he can stay home! I plan to go somewhere without him. He can learn to be on his own for the weekend!" Rachel responded, "Good idea. Go away for a change!"

The waitress brought the two orders of fish and chips as well as the clam chowder to Sue and Rachel's table. They began eating their tasty lunch. They dipped their buttered fish in fish sauce. They munched on their French fries and sipped their coffee. After they were done eating their lunch they continued sipping their coffee while they continued to visit.

Rachel began talking about herself. She said, "I met a guy recently who seems charming and available. I have hesitated to go out with him. He works down the street from our firm. He hasn't asked me out yet. What should I do?" Sue looked interested. She answered, "Why don't you ask him out for a date?" Rachel replied, "I don't want to appear too aggressive. He might think I am coming on too strong!" Sue responded, "How are you going to get to know him better if you don't take the initiative? He may be flattered that you have asked him for a date. Don't be afraid, Rachel to ask him out. Besides, what have you got to lose? He may accept your date. So, please go ask him soon."

Rachel looked perplexed and worried. She replied, "Maybe I will ask him out. I will have to get up some courage to ask him." The lunch hour was nearly up. Sue and Rachel paid for their lunch. They walked back to their office and resumed working at their desks.

When the mid afternoon break came the office workers went to the lounge room to have coffee and to visit. Sue, Mary Jean and Rachel sat near each other. They had become very well acquainted. Other office workers were sitting near them. Cheryl was sitting nearest to Rachel, Sue and Mary Jean. Cheryl began unwinding by saying, "I'm tired! I am ready to go home now! We have two more hours after break time to work! I am so bored with all these repeated job assignments. I can't keep up with my boss when I am taking quick notes when he dictates letters!"

Sue, Mary Jean and Rachel were listening to Cheryl with sympathy. Sue responded, "Did you sleep well last night?" Cheryl replied, "Not really. Maybe this is why I can't keep up!" Mary Jean responded, "I didn't sleep well last night. There was so much noise outside. Sirens were going off in the street. I am ready to go home, too! I need a nap!" Rachel was listening. She decided not to say anything. She sipped her coffee. She was thinking about how she was going to approach the appealing guy down the street to ask him for a date. Coffee break was over. Everyone went back to work.

Finally, it was time to go home at 5 p.m. Sue, Mary Jean, Rachel, Cheryl and the other eight office workers in the office stepped out of their office to go home. Each of them went to their homes by bus or car. Rachel walked down the street to a shop where the appealing, dark haired, brown eyed, tall and slender man worked.

Rachel got up enough courage to walk up to him. She approached him with an air of false confidence. She smiled at him. Rachel said, "Hi. Do you remember me? I came to this store the other day. I saw you then." The store manager looked at Rachel with curiosity. He answered, "I don't recall seeing you. Can I help you?" Rachel began to feel insecure. She felt uncomfortable about asking this fellow for a date because he didn't even remember her.

Rachel looked at the store manager with an uncertain expression. She said, "I bought some office supplies here the other day." The store manager looked at Rachel in a manner of trying to recall seeing her. He responded, "I think I remember seeing you the other day. We have a lot of customers who come into our store. Do you want to purchase anything?"

Rachel sensed that this appealing man was being business-like only. He didn't seem to be personable to her. Rachel thought about what Sue had told her earlier in the day. What did she have to lose by asking him out on a date? So, Rachel courageously said, "Would you like to go out on a date this Friday night?" The store manager looked at Rachel with a surprised expression. He replied, "Thank you for asking. I can't go on a date with you on Friday night. I am married. My wife wouldn't like it if I saw another woman."

Rachel felt suddenly despondent. The appealing man wasn't wearing a wedding ring. She had assumed that he was single. She said, "Oh. I didn't realize that you are married. Well, I guess I better go." Rachel walked out of the store. She took a bus to her apartment. She thought about how she had taken the initiative to ask a stranger out.

The next day at the mid morning coffee break Rachel spoke to Sue about her experience with the appealing, store manager. Sue responded. "At least you tried to have a date with him. You found out he was married. Don't let this experience discourage you from meeting someone else." Rachel looked at Sue with respect. She said, "I won't. Maybe I will meet someone else soon." The office workers went on gossiping while they had their coffee break.

Fiction

FIFTY-SEVEN

Picnic At The Lake

Peggy and Charles Minnow planned a picnic at a beautiful, deep blue lake twenty-five miles south from their home. They packed a delicious picnic lunch which included baked chicken, potato salad, cole slaw, sliced tomatoes and cucumbers, whole wheat homemade bread with butter, chocolate, chip cookies, bottled cider and tapioca pudding.

Peggy and Charles placed their picnic basket in the trunk of their car. They began their trip to the beautiful, deep blue lake which was one of the largest, longest lakes in their state. Peggy and Charles lived in California. The largest lake is Lake Tahoe. They enjoyed viewing evergreen trees such as pine, fir and spruce trees. The fragrance of the evergreen pine, fir and spruce needles and bark of these trees enthralled Peggy and Charles as they drove by on the road to their destination.

Within an hour Peggy and Charles had arrived at Lake Tahoe. They stopped in an ideal location at Lake Tahoe. They parked their car near the lake. There were pine, fir and spruce trees near the lake. Charles placed a blanket on the ground close to the beautiful lake. Then Charles carried the picnic basket to the blanket and laid it down.

Peggy and Charles looked around to enjoy the view of Lake Tahoe. They sat down on the blanket. Peggy took the picnic food out of the basket. Peggy put baked chicken, potato salad, cole slaw, cut tomatoes and cucumbers on two plates. She battered whole wheat bread. She handed Charles a plate of food. She received the second plate of food.

The Minnows enjoyed their picnic lunch. They observed boats on the lake while they were eating. Some people were sailing in sailboats. Some people were water skiing on the lake. The deep blue lake was interesting to view. Peggy and Charles ate tapioca pudding and chocolate chip cookies for dessert. They drank cider.

Then Peggy cleaned up the plates and put extra food away. The food was put back in the trunk of the Minnow's car. Peggy saved the scraps to feed squirrels which were scampering around nearby under the pine trees. Peggy put the food scraps such as bread crumbs, potato salad and cut veggies on the ground for the squirrels. The squirrels came up quickly and nibbled at the food scraps. Peggy and Charles enjoyed feeding the squirrels. After the picnic area was cleaned up Peggy and Charles went walking around the edge of the lake. There was no beach sand. There was a pathway near the edge of the lake. Peggy and Charles walked along the lake for several miles. They observed rippling water. Some ducks were moving gracefully in the lake.

As Peggy and Charles walked they saw flocks of birds fly by. They heard meadowlarks and blue jays chirping and chattering around them. Suddenly some deer and their fawns meandered in the nearby pine trees. They stopped to observe the deer who were nibbling on grass and pine needles. The fawns also nibbled grass and pine needles. The deer saw Peggy and Charles staring at them. They went on eating for a period of time. Finally they walked away and disappeared. Peggy and Charles decided to turn around to head back to the area where their car was parked. They walked several miles back. They felt the warm sunshine on their faces and bodies. It was a very pleasant day.

While Peggy and Charles were walking towards their picnic area and car they continued to observe passengers walking along the edge of the lake. A couple walked near Peggy and Charles. They appeared friendly as they approached Peggy and Charles. The lady and man, who appeared middle aged, greeted Peggy and Charles. Then the couple stopped to talk to Peggy and Charles.

The lady said, "Hello. Nice day for a walk. Have you been walking very long?" Charles replied, "We have walked over 4 miles so far. Have you been walking very long?" The lady, who was called Shirley replied, "My husband and I started walking three hours ago. We have walked 6 miles already." Peggy responded, "You have been walking even more miles than we have. Do you walk along this lake often?" Shirley answered, "My husband and I walk around this lake just about every day to exercise and enjoy this lake." Charles responded, do you live near Lake Tahoe?" Shirley's husband, Trenton, replied, "We walk every day to keep healthy and strong. Do you live near here?" Peggy replied, "No. we live 45 miles away from here." Shirley responded, "I'm glad you are walking near this beautiful lake today? Maybe we will see you again if you decide to come back to Lake Tahoe.

The couple continued to walk along the edge of the lake. Peggy and Charles continued their walk back to their car. They thought about the couple who walked near this large lake everyday. When Peggy and Charles returned to their home they thought about their opportunity to visit Lake Tahoe more often so they could go walking again to enjoy the magnificent views and exercise to keep strong and healthy.

Fiction

FIFTY-EIGHT

The Special Message

Rebecca Gillman grew up in New York City in Greenwich Village. She was surrounded by poets, scholars, artists and musicians. Rebecca attended lectures at the community center and at church. Rebecca also went to the University of New York to attend lectures.

One afternoon Rebecca attended a special lecture in a big auditorium at the University of New York. The auditorium filled up with over one thousand people. Rebecca sat towards the front of the auditorium closer to the lecture podium. Once everyone had arrived the lecture began at approximately 2:10 p.m.

A lady dressed in an attractive, lavender suit walked on the stage to the lectern. She had a folder in her hands. She placed the folder on the podium. She appeared around 45 years old with strawberry blonde hair and blue eyes. She introduced herself. "Good afternoon, everyone. I am Dr. Joyce Cook. Today I will speak about CAUSES AND REMEDIES FOR RELIGIOUS CONFLICTS. You probably wonder why I selected this topic. There are many religious beliefs in the world. People believe in very different values and beliefs. Christians are different than the Jewish religion. Christians believe in Jesus Christ as Lord of Lords. Jews believe in Jehovah God. They do not believe in Jesus Christ as Lord of Lords. Moslems believe Jesus Christ was a prophet. Mohamed continued as the next prophet after Jesus Christ. Saint Gabriel spoke to Mohamed and instructed him. Many people have followed the Islamic religion. They pray

Cecelia Frances Page

five times a day and bow before Allah. They believe they will go to Mecca someday if they live by the Moslem religion."

Dr. Joyce Cook paused and then continued speaking at the podium on the stage in the big auditorium. The audience was waiting quietly to hear her continue her lecture. Dr. Cook began speaking again. She said, "Many people do not believe in the Moslem religion. They believe Moslems take away the freedom from Moslem women. Many Middle Eastern women who are Moslems must wear veils over their faces. They are required to be escorted when they step out of their homes. Moslem men make all major decisions while Moslem women must obey their Moslem husbands. They are not allowed to make important decisions."

Dr. Joyce Cook paused for a few seconds before speaking again. Then she continued speaking. She said, "Individuals who are Christians believe in equality of women and black people. The Moslem religion causes lack of freedom between men and women. This is considered to be unjust and unfair in the West. How can Moslem women become liberated? They need the support of political leaders to be able to become liberated. Women in the Middle East should be free to vote for changes which will bring about true freedom and liberation in their personal lives and culture. Religious freedom is important."

Dr. Joyce Cook continued speaking for another twenty minutes or more before she concluded her lecture. Rebecca was impressed with this special message. The audience applauded because she had completed her speech. Dr. Cook walked off the stage. The audience began leaving the big auditorium. Rebecca Stillman walked out of the University auditorium. She thought about Dr. Joyce Cook's lecture about religious differences and conflicts. She planned to come back to the University in two weeks to attend another lecture.

FIFTY-NINE

Chinese New Year

Chinese New Year changes every year. This year will be on February 14th. This coming year will be the tiger. Each year is a different animal. There has been the year of the lion, snake, rat, boar, horse and elephant, etc.

Astrological signs are determined by the year a person is born. Individuals are more compatible with certain signs. Individuals may not be compatible with certain signs.

During Chinese New Year many Chinese people celebrate. They dress up and walk in parades. Usually a large manmade dragon is moved around in the street in a big parade.

Chinese fireworks are displayed in the night sky to bring in the Chinese New Year each year. Chinese New Year is celebrated with feasts and singing. It is a special event every year.

Nonfiction

SIXTY

How To Live In Harmony With Nature

Living in harmony with nature is important. When individuals sit outside to bask in the sun they are able to feel the healing rays which produce vitamins to strengthen one's body. To smell the fragrance of living trees, flowers and bushes uplifts the body and mind

When we send out a harmonious vibration to all living creatures, plants and water it helps the nature elementals to perform their task in supplying enough protection and energy wherever fire, air, water and earth are needed. Each elemental serves in the nature kingdom.

We need to take care of our environment. Every tree, flower, grass and animal need a safe, healthy place to survive. Pollution in the air, water and earth (soil) cause trees, flowers, grass and animal life to die out or to become unhealthy.

Agriculturalists need to replenish and enrich soil before planting new crops. Air pollutants need to be eliminated in the air. Pollutants must be kept out of the water in the world. Harmony can be established in nature with clean air, water and soil.

When enough food is available for animals and enough food is grown for the world's people there will be more harmony in nature around the world. More beautiful gardens and growing crops add to the environment. Gardens and crops need to be watered and fed nutrients to be healthy and to grow well. Avoid stepping on plants. Keep wild animals from stepping all over your gardens and crops. Plants can be destroyed easily by lawn mowers, tractors and large animals that trample on them.

You could fence in your garden and crops. Plenty of sunshine and water are needed to help gardens and crops to grow. Avoid playing harsh, discordant music near your gardens. Plants respond to sounds. Play harmonious music near your garden and agricultural crops.

The American Indians were close to nature. They communicated with nature spirits. They believed in rain spirits, sun spirits and fire spirits. Indians spoke to animals and plants. American Indians didn't waste anything in nature. Every part of an animal used for food also could be used for their skins, bones and internal parts.

Skins were used to make clothes, blankets and carpets. Bones are used to make needles to sew with. Bones were used to make tools and weapons.

Animals such as horses are well cared for by American Indians. Horses were important for the American Indians to use to ride for transportation. Horses were fed and groomed.

American Indians hunted for only what they needed for food and other reasons. We should take care of our pets and livestock. Animals need tender, loving care. They need enough food and water. Some animals need personal attention. Cats and dogs like to be petted and spoken to. Horses, donkeys and ponies also like to be petted as well as fed personally by people.

Nature is preserved when climates are pleasant. When temperatures are not too cold or not too hot, plants and animals survive much better. Living species and plants respond better to a good climate.

We need to maintain harmony with all living creatures, plants and elementals to help our planet, Earth thrive with natural resources and abundance.

Nonfiction

SIXTY-ONE

Making Enemies Our Friends

We all encounter enemies during our lifetime. Why do we have enemies? Who are our enemies? How can we make enemies our friends? These are questions which will be answered in this chapter. An enemy is someone who deliberately causes harm, disharmony and causes a lot of pain and unnecessary suffering to someone he or she hates and despises. An enemy is someone who cannot be trusted. This person will attack a person he or she dislikes intensely.

How can you make an enemy a friend? You need to forgive evil thoughts and actions created by an enemy. Learn to help an enemy overcome hatred, avarice, resentment, jealousy and fear. Misunderstandings can be cleared up. Someone may become your friend in time if you keep finding ways to create a friendship. Learn to understand why an enemy became so hateful, resentful and jealous of you. This person is focusing on negative emotions. He or she has not learned to raise their emotions to a much higher level. An enemy has not focused on loving, accepting and forgiving you for their own wrongdoing and negative actions as well as your reaction to their behavior.

You must find a way to arouse your enemy to change his or her attitudes towards you. You need to perform kind and loving actions to warm your enemy's heart. You need to prove to your enemy that you are not his or her enemy. Tell this person you want to be his or her friend and maintain a positive and friendly manner. In time your enemy may become your friend.

Fiction

SIXTY-TWO

Fragile Relationships

Relationships with other individuals can be fragile. Individuals are sensitive and can be easily hurt. What we say to others can affect them emotionally. If we insult and name call our friends, spouse and acquaintances they may turn against us. We should think before we speak to others.

To speak falsely and critically against our neighbors can cause them to suffer and have them experience unnecessary pain. We need to be thoughtful and act with kindness to others, especially our loved ones.

Jacquelyn Miller lived with her mother and father until she was eighteen. She recalled how her parents argued frequently. They attacked each other with unkind words and unpleasant vocal tones. Jacquelyn's mother was sullen for days after her husband argued over petty issues. Joe was upset when she overheard her parents bickering. She didn't understand why they behaved this way.

When Jacquelyn was 18 years old she went away to college. She attended the University of Colorado. She was glad to get away from her parents. She stayed at the University dorm. She shared a dorm room with another college student. Her dorm mate, Jean, was 19 years old. Jean was a sophomore in college.

Jacquelyn had a single bed in one corner plus a desk nearby. Jean's bed was in the other corner. Her desk was near her bed. Jacquelyn and Jean had two separate closets to store their clothes and other belongings.

Jacquelyn had never lived in a dorm, especially with someone she didn't know. She tried to get along with Jean by speaking with courtesy and thoughtfulness. At first her pleasant, courteous approach worked. She was getting along with Jean.

Jacquelyn enrolled in four classes the first quarter. She took 12 units. She was very busy with her college courses. She had a lot of reading to do plus research papers to complete. So, Jacquelyn was very occupied with her college studies.

Then, one day when Jacquelyn came back to her dorm room she walked in and Jean was gone. All of Jean's belongings were gone. Jacquelyn had not been told that she was moving away. A new dorm mate was sent to share the dorm room with Jacquelyn.

The new dorm mate was Delphine. Delphine was 21 years old. She was a senior in college. Jacquelyn observed that Delphine smoked and she turned on a radio when she studied. The radio music was loud and distracting. Jacquelyn tried to study. However, the radio music was too distracting. Jacquelyn was unable to study at her desk in her dorm room.

Jacquelyn was put in a position to tell Delphine that she couldn't concentrate on her studies with the radio on. Delphine reacted in a negative manner. Delphine said, "I have a right to turn on my radio if I want to listen to it!" Jacquelyn responded, "I wouldn't ask you to turn off your radio if I could study." Delphine answered, "I need to listen to music on the radio to relax."

Jacquelyn remained silent in order to avoid an argument with Delphine. She knew that arguing with her probably wouldn't solve the problem. Jacquelyn didn't want to have a negative relationship with her dorm mate. Relationships can be fragile when arguments begin.

Jacquelyn decided to purchase some earplugs to wear so that she could study. Jacquelyn was allergic to Delphine's smoking in their dorm room. She finally told her that smoke caused her to cough and sneeze. Delpine refused to stop smoking.

Jacquelyn decided that she would have to request another dorm room with someone who didn't smoke as well as play a radio during study time. Jacquelyn wanted to do well in college and to remain healthy. So, Jacquelyn went to the dorm room coordinator to change rooms. The dorm room coordinator checked the dorm room book for any vacancies. She told Jacqueline that all the dorm rooms were presently occupied. Perhaps there would be an opening the next quarter. Jacquelyn would have to wait or find a place to stay outside the University dorm.

Jacquelyn became despondent about her present situation which was caused by her thoughtless, dorm mate, Delphine. Jacquelyn would have to tolerate Delphine or find another place to live. Jacquelyn decided to find another place to live. She looked in newspapers for a room to rent. She circled different advertisements. Then she went to look at several rooms near the University.

Jacquelyn finally selected a room in someone's home. She had kitchen privileges. This room was $575 a month. Her dorm room was $400. Jacquelyn would have to pay $175 more a month. So, Jacqueline looked for a part time job in order to pay for her new room.

Jacquelyn was happier because her room was comfortable. It was quiet in the house and no one smoked. Jacquelyn was able to study much better. She didn't cough and sneeze anymore. Jacquelyn was able to maintain a good relationship with an elderly lady who was pleasant and mature. This elderly lady was easy to get along with. She had a sense of humor and she was thoughtful. Jacquelyn was grateful to have a better place to live with someone who she could have a positive relationship with.

SIXTY-THREE

Awaken To Spiritual Consciousness

Awakening to spiritual awareness is an uplifting and very worthwhile experience. Every higher thought allows one's soul to become illuminated. Illumination is the way to Christ consciousness.

Every spiritual guru and world teacher has experienced spiritual illumination. What is illumination? Illumination is the light of God with wisdom one listens to with the inner voice of the higher self. Illuminated souls have remarkable thoughts which enlighten them.

By awakening to spiritual consciousness enlightened souls are able to help awaken other souls to higher consciousness. Enlightened, spiritual leaders such as Jesus Christ, Buddha, Yogananda, Mother Mary, Krishna and others have awakened their followers to spiritual consciousness.

Souls who don't search for truth and who don't seek wisdom and spiritual awareness may have to reincarnate many times until they learn to become God realized through higher consciousness. Each soul must overcome the veil of illusion and maya in order to become spiritually aware. The veil of illusion creates more karma known as cause and effect.

Negative karma must be dissolved in the subconscious. Akashic records store memories of negative experiences which must be transmuted so each soul can be liberated from human desires and darkness. At least 51% of human karma must be dissolved and transmuted so a soul can transcend into a higher plane.

Spiritual awareness is the way to the path to God reality. Each soul must tread a path of discipleship by living by the Golden Rule and brotherhood and sisterhood. We are allowed to make our own choices. The kind of choices we make determine what will happen to us. Positive choices can help us live better lives. Negative choices cause us to slow down our spiritual progress. We need to make wise choices in order to make spiritual progress.

Nonfiction

SIXTY-FOUR

Life As A Vegan

A vegan is a person who does not eat any meat, fish and dairy products. A vegan does not eat cheese, butter, yogurt, ice cream, tartar sauce, or grease, lard, mayonnaise, and cream. Vegans do not drink milk or eat cottage cheese.

So, what do vegans eat? They eat soy beans, red beans, navy beans, lima beans, black beans, garbanzo beans, lentils, brown and white rice, noodles and spaghetti made without eggs. Vegans eat a wide variety of vegetables and fruit. They usually eat organically grown vegetables and fruit.

Vegans drink different, fruit juices such as orange juice, pineapple juice, papaya juice, grapefruit juice and prune juice, etc. Vegans especially enjoy eating bananas, oranges, apples, grapes, grapefruit, peaches, pears, lemons, pineapples and other fresh fruits. They eat fresh lettuce, tomatoes, carrots, green beans, squash, cabbage, onions, green, red and yellow peppers, parsley, cucumbers, sprouts, spinach, brussel sprouts, etc.

Generally, a vegan eats raw fruits for breakfast. Fruit juice may be consumed at breakfast. Then a vegan may prepare a raw salad of dark green lettuce with sprouts, onions, garlic, carrots and tomatoes. A natural salad dressing is prepared with vinaigrette and lemon juice.

Then a vegan may eat sprouted bread with cut vegetables such as sliced tomatoes, sprouts and green peppers. Later, spaghetti is prepared with egg-free spaghetti, noodles and tomato sauce. Brown rice is also eaten. Potatoes, spirulina, tofu, wheat grass juice, super blue-green algae, wheat germ, flaxseed oil and organic vitamin supplements are also popular. Daily complete protein is obtained by Nutri-Soy organic, natural, non-GMO, protein powder. One glass of this beverage contains 100% of the daily requirements of protein and vitamins A, B6, B12, D and E, as well as 11 other vital nutrients. Certain tofu and soy products contain complete, daily calcium. Vital brain nutrients come from flaxseed. Skeptics believe vegans do not receive enough protein and calcium. They should remember that the biggest and strongest animals in the world are vegans! These animals include elephants, giraffes, apes, bulls and the tallest, extinct dinosaurs.

For dessert a vegan may eat health food cookies, nuts, soy ice cream, and other tasty non-dairy items. Health food stores offer many delicious vegan deserts. Non-refined, pure, non-chemical, organic, raw sugar cane is a health food! When combined with organic chocolate it has health benefits. Raw nuts may be consumed at snack time with tofu for additional protein. Wheat grass juice and sprouts also contain much protein.

A vegan can enjoy a well-balanced diet of nutritional, organic foods. Vegans are able to eat enough protein foods to remain healthy. Vegans tend to be healthier than individuals who eat meat and fish because vegans do not eat dead matter, greasy foods, high cholesterol foods and manmade, processed foods that are genetically engineered, artificially with toxic chemicals added. Pure vegans avoid chemical preservatives. A large amount of restaurant and market food contains foods raised with genetic, DNA alterations (GMO) which was proven in scientific experiments to be dangerous. Real organic food does not contain GMO. Most livestock and poultry are raised with genetic engineered GMO, as well as eating chemically treated meals and hormone injections dangerous to humans.

Vegans are able to eat an interesting variety of foods which are very good for their bodies. They generally live much longer than people who eat meat. More and more people should become vegans.

Research has found that pets raised on natural, organic, non-processed foods live twice as long as those raised on the popular, packaged and canned pet foods.

SIXTY-FIVE

Twin Flames

Twin flames are two souls who were created at the same time. They share the same God flames of masculine and feminine polarities on the higher planes. They affect each others karma by merging together through the higher self or real self.

It may take many lifetimes for twin flames to evolve so that one twin flame can help the other twin flame to evolve. The ultimate goal is for twin flames to ascend and for them to serve one another. They incarnate many times to work out karma together. Twin flames are merged to serve in the Great Central Sun.

Mark and Elizabeth Clare Prophet claimed to be twin flames. They worked together in The Summit Lighthouse as spiritual gurus. Both of them shared karma in other embodiments as well as the present incarnation. It is believed that Mark Prophet ascended in 1973. Elizabeth Clare Prophet passed away in 2009. They both contributed spiritual awareness as spiritual leaders. St. Germain and Portia are twin flames. Both have ascended and they are One on the higher planes.

Everyone has a twin flame. When souls are more evolved they will recognize their twin flame. They will feel more complete when they consciously work with their twin flame.